Contents

FOREWORD

When I first came to London, I soon realised from my English friends that their concept of Chinese food often tended to be a familiar stereotype – 'Chinese' equated to one of the usual take-away or late-night, post-pub cheap and easy fill-ups, accompanied by pints of lager. It would be fair to say that the dishes offered were a kind of ersatz Cantonese cooking. Dishes such as Chop Suey and Chow Mein featured, which in reality owed more to Brooklyn than Beijing. Most people, not having visited China or Hong Kong, had no idea what was authentic and what wasn't, and probably weren't interested anyway.

Since then, there has been a huge growth in the popularity of Oriental cuisine. Hopefully this book will demonstrate what a great variety of appetising dishes are available.

There are many cookery books obtainable in every bookshop and indeed this is yet another one. However, what we are setting out to achieve here is threefold: firstly, to provide a straightforward textbook for anyone interested in Chinese cuisine; secondly, to remind us that China is a vast and fascinating country with a great panoply of cuisines, beyond but including Cantonese, in each case influenced by the climate, terrain and available produce; and thirdly, to show that many delicious dishes are quite simple to prepare and inexpensive, relying on the quality of the ingredients and some basic techniques, all readily explained in this book.

Importantly, though, once you have understood the basic skills, there is enormous scope for improvisation. Cooking is a creative art and Chinese ingredients very much lend themselves to this. The art of innovation comes from within yourself and you can express your own personality through your own interpretation of recipes.

My co-author, Norman Fu, who is a lecturer in Chinese Cookery at Westminster Kingsway College, has tested and can vouch for all the recipes. The students, who are from diverse backgrounds and nationalities, found them easy to follow. The School was established in 1999 at Westminster College in London and many acclaimed chefs have been trained there. You don't have to be Chinese to be able to produce excellent Chinese food!

Incidentally, it is worth mastering the art of using chopsticks – like swimming or riding a bike, once learnt you can always do it! Remember however that you should never use one chopstick to spear food; this is like using a knife to eat from – it is just not done.

Christine Yau

ACKNOWLEDGEMENTS

For me, writing this book has been an interesting experience, much like my first year in teaching! There are a few people that must be acknowledged, as they have been influential in the writing of this book and my development as a teacher. First of all, my father, Kwun Fu, who taught me everything I know, and my mother Shui Ying Fu, my brother Raymond and my sisters Liza and Linda, who all encouraged me that my destiny lay with food and not chemistry. Secondly, Martyn Wagner, who hired me to teach at the former Westminster College, and Kevin Selwood, Louise Jordan, Barry Jones and Bernard Vokes, all of whom helped me the most in my transition from Chef to Chef lecturer. And finally, all my colleagues in the Culinary Arts division for their support and encouragement.

Norman Fu

I would like to express my sincere thanks to the following for their invaluable help with the book – Mr Tang, Lee Kum Kee, Mary Soong and everyone at Westminster Kingsway College.

Christine Yau

The authors and publishers would like to thank the following:

For assistance on the photoshoot – James Newell (photographer), Ian Fenn, and Chi Hing Leung, and to Gary Hunter (Head of Culinary Arts, Westminster Kingsway College) for allowing use of the college facilities.

For permission to reproduce copyright material – © Fritz Hoffmann, documentCHINA: page viii; © Dean Conger/CORBIS: page xv; Mr C.T.Tang: page xvii.

Every effort has been made to obtain necessary permission with reference to copyright material. The publishers apologise if inadvertently any sources remain unacknowledged and will be glad to make the necessary arrangements at the earliest opportunity.

Please note: All recipes serve 4 unless stated otherwise.

INTRODUCTION

Many of you will have seen Ang Lee's film, *Eat Drink Man Woman*, but some of you probably don't know that the origin of the quotation was the Chinese philosopher Mencius, the successor of Confucius. He argued that humans are all born good, but are made better or worse by their environments.

This quotation also summarises the Chinese attitude to food in life, for while it is generally assumed that most people eat in order to live, the Chinese live in order to eat. Whether or not Chinese cuisine is the greatest in the world is debatable, but no one can dispute the fact that, when it is done correctly, following a set of rules and principles adapted by chefs and cooks throughout China for centuries, it is the most exciting food available today.

When I first started teaching at Ken Lo's Memories of China Cookery School more than twenty years ago, there was not a single textbook for Chinese cuisine in the English language on the market. All the cookery books published in the West at that time were written by non-professionals, mainly for home cooks. In **International Cuisine: China** we have a textbook written by two professionals – Christine Yau, the much-respected restaurateur who has a deep understanding of all things relating to Chinese food culture, and Norman Fu, a lecturer at London's Westminster Kingsway School of Chinese Cookery. It is written specifically for the serious-minded student, yet it should also appeal to a wider public, since all the recipes are written with clear and straightforward instructions. Another unique feature of this book is that the recipes are grouped under the different cooking methods rather than the ingredients used, thus avoiding the tedium of too much unnecessary repetition of step-by-step cooking instructions for each individual recipe.

Before you commence any serious cooking, I strongly urge you to read this short introduction, as well as the sections on cutting techniques, cooking methods and basic ingredients that precede the actual recipes, in order to acquaint yourself with the fundamental history and philosophy of the Chinese cuisine; it is the Chinese philosophy that provides the foundation, while the cooking techniques are the bricks and mortar. Without philosophy to give it shape, Chinese food is shallow; without technique, it falls apart. It is like a special house that one cannot hope to build from the pinnacles downwards.

The Chinese prefer their seafood to be really, really fresh

A brief history of Chinese cuisine

China is an ancient civilisation and Chinese cuisine developed with it through its 5,000 years of recorded history.

It can safely be assumed that in the remote, primitive beginnings of mankind's existence, our ancestors across the face of the earth all led a life eating what has been described as 'raw meat with fur and blood'. There was no such thing as cooking until much later, when fire was discovered, and food was then 'cooked', although without any seasonings to speak of.

So it was many, many millennia later that cultivated plants and domesticated animals began to provide the bulk foodstuff for people, and the gathering of wild fruits, nuts, berries and other edible materials as supplements to the human diet became commonplace. Only then was a different 'food culture' said to have been created, with regional variations, which was based on the natural distribution of plants and animals from area to area.

Not until much later, when early civilisation began to develop in some parts of the world, did a form of cooking style start to emerge. Eventually, we had three main types of cuisine: Chinese or Oriental (which includes practically all of South-East Asia and Japan); Central Asia or Middle Eastern (which now includes the Indian sub-continent and most parts of Africa as well as the Caribbean); and European or Western (which, nowadays, also includes the New Worlds). Each of these cuisines not only has its own distinct cooking styles, but also the way the foods are prepared before cooking and the manner in which the meals are served differ. For instance, Orientals traditionally use chopsticks as eating utensils, while Asians and Africans usually use their fingers, and Westerners always use knives and forks.

Some of the most conspicuous traces of early Chinese culture have been found at sites that lie along the valley of the Yellow River in northern China, which is why this area is known as the cradle of Chinese civilisation. Archaeological finds have provided ample evidence to show that in 5000 BC, the inhabitants of northern China had begun to settle down, farm and make painted pottery to use as eating and cooking vessels. Woks and Chinese cleavers were in use as far back as the Bronze Age (around 2500 BC)!

We have to wait until around 2000 BC, when written records first appeared, before we can piece together a reasonably complete picture of the dietary habits of the ancient Chinese. We learn that the people of the Shang dynasty (from 1600–1066 BC) grew millet, wheat, barley and rice, and they fermented their grains to make some form of alcoholic beverages, and that during the Zhou dynasty (1066–221 BC), soy beans were added to the Chinese diet. By this time, the Chinese already practised the art of blending different flavours by using several ingredients in one dish, and they cut and prepared their foodstuffs before cooking them – two of the main characteristics of Chinese cuisine.

Chinese cuisine has gone through thousands of years of refinement and development. Man began to cook by wrapping food in mud and straw before roasting; then roasting food directly over the fire; then slicing the meat and roasting the sliced meat on a spit; then cooking the food in a vessel with water to boil; then putting food over water to steam it. Oil in cooking came much later. Before the Han dynasty (206 BC–220 AD) only animal fat was used, and in the late Han dynasty plant seeds were pressed to extract their oil. The use of these oils for cooking accelerated the development of culinary art. The Chinese learnt first to fry, and then to deep-fry and stir-fry over a blazing fire.

With the increasing variety and abundance of foodstuffs, and progress in experimentation and study, Chinese cuisine has been perfected through the ages. We have written proof that as early as the Warring States period (475–221 BC) during the Zhou dynasty, flavourings such as soy sauce, vinegar, salt, plum jam, molasses and honey were used to make the dishes taste sweet and sour! Cooking techniques were complicated and numerous. An essay on culinary theory entitled 'Chapter on Natural Tastes' appeared in the *Annals of Lu*. It pointed out that the control of the flame and mastery of seasonings were crucial to good cooking. These, along with the proper cooking time, would eliminate any unpleasant odour and bring out the best flavours in food.

It was during the Han dynasty that China established trade with central Asia, and this contact brought Buddhism to China. In the year 138 BC, the great adventurer Zhang Jian (?–114 BC) was sent to the 'western regions' (which cover an area spreading as far west as the Persian Gulf) as China's envoy. He was credited with introducing all sorts of exotic food into China, including alfalfa, grapes, walnuts, sesame, onions, peas, broad beans, coriander, pepper and cucumber. Then around 100 BC, the first traders took the historic Silk Road through central Asia, bringing new spices and vegetables to China. (To this day, spinach is called 'Persian lettuce' in Chinese.) Meanwhile, beancurd (*tofu*) and many bean products were invented in China, and with this increase in the availability of a variety of foodstuffs, so cooking techniques also developed.

In AD 166, the first trade link between the Roman Empire and China was recorded. The barrier that lay between the great civilisations of the East and West was lifted, and not only merchandise, but also philosophies were exchanged, with repercussions beyond measure resulting.

By the time of the Tang dynasty (AD 618–907) and the Song dynasty (960–1279), China was the most powerful empire in the East. Domestic stability and a flourishing culture attracted many people from other countries and they came to learn. Culinary arts were flourishing as well. Not only were colour, aroma and flavour important, the shape and texture of a dish had become essential to gourmet cooking.

During the Ming (1368–1644) and Qing (Manchu) (1644–1912) dynasties, the development of sea transportation brought such delicacies as bird's nests, shark's fins and sea cucumbers to the banquet tables. These delicacies were usually preserved in dried form and had to be soaked and reconstituted in water before cooking. The skill of preparing and cooking them was specialised, and the chefs of the Ming and Qing dynasties mastered these to perfection. These delicacies are regarded as texture food, for although they are rather bland in taste, they require the correct balance of seasonings to complement the texture in each of them.

In the Qing dynasty, a grand Manchu-Han banquet that lasted three days was typically made up of six major courses, six minor courses, four accompanying courses, two or three desserts, and 24 trays (4 of dried fruits, 4 of preserved fruits, 8 of cold dishes and 4 of hot dishes). In addition, the guests were served appetisers and two courses of tea before the meal. The banquets were extravagant and wasteful, but they brought together the best of Han and Manchu cooking, and were a magnificent display of the exquisiteness of Chinese cuisine.

The principles of Chinese cuisine

History and tradition are not the only characteristic features of Chinese cuisine. It is also closely related to Chinese culture. As stated at the beginning of this introduction, food is part of the way of life, strongly influenced by the two early philosophies of Taoism and Confucianism.

Both Lao-Tze (c 605–530 BC), the founder of Taoism, and Confucius (551–479 BC) lived and taught during the late Zhou dynasty (770–249 BC). It was the Taoist School (*Tao* being the Chinese word for 'way', the mystic path of righteousness that lies at the core of Lao-Tze's teaching) that developed the hygienic and nutritional science of food, while Confucianism was more concerned with the art of cooking.

Confucius stressed social ritual as a teacher of virtue. It was he who laid down the rules to be followed in recipes, and the correct custom and etiquette of the table, which, to a certain extent, are still being adhered to even to this day.

As mentioned earlier, the main distinctive feature of Chinese cuisine is the emphasis on the harmonious blending of colour, aroma, flavour, shape and texture, both in a single dish and in a course of dishes.

Colour 色 (*Se*): Each ingredient has its own natural colour. Certain items change their colour after cooking, so the cook should bear this in mind when selecting different ingredients for blending of colours: is the dish to have contrasting or complementary colours? And what are the colours of other dishes that are being served at the same time? All these points should be taken into consideration when planning a menu.

Aroma 香 (*Xiang*): Again, each ingredient has its own aroma or fragrance: some sharp, some subtle. Most fish and meat have a rather strong smell and require an agent to suppress it and to enhance its cooked aroma. The Chinese use rice wine and spirits in cooking for this purpose; other much-used seasonings are spring onions, ginger, garlic and peppers.

Flavour 味 (*Wei*): Flavour is closely related to aroma and colour, and the principle of blending complementary flavours is a fundamental one: the different ingredients must not be mixed indiscriminately; and the matching of flavours should follow a set pattern and be controlled, not casual. Some cooks like to mix contrasting flavours and unrelated textures; others prefer the matching of similar flavours and colours. Some wish the flavour of each ingredient to be preserved, others believe in the infusion of flavours. The blending of different flavours known as *tiao-wei* is itself a fine art, and in this lies the central principle of harmony.

Shape 形 (*Xing*): The cutting of ingredients is important in achieving the proper cooking effect. Slices are matched with slices, shreds with shreds, cubes with cubes, chunks with chunks, and so on. This is not merely for the sake of appearance, which is an important element of Chinese cuisine, but also because ingredients of the same size and shape require about the same amount of time in cooking.

Texture 質地 (*Zhidi*): A dish may have just one, or several, contrasting textures, such as tenderness, crispness, crunchiness, smoothness and softness. The textures to be avoided are sogginess, stringiness and hardness. To achieve the correct texture in a dish – the hallmark of authentic Chinese cuisine – the most important points to observe here are the degree of heat and the duration of cooking, known by the Chinese term *huohou* 火侯, meaning 'heat and timing'.

The desired texture(s) in any dish can only be achieved by the right cooking methods. The size and shape of the cut ingredient must, first of all, be suitable for the particular method of cooking. For instance, ingredients for quick stir-frying should be cut into small, thin slices, shreds or small cubes, never large, thick chunks.

You will have noticed that a Chinese dish is usually made up of more than one ingredient; this is because when a single item is cooked on its own, it lacks contrast and therefore harmony. For centuries, Chinese cooks have understood the importance of the harmonious balance in blending different flavours. The principle of blending complementary or contrasting colours, flavours and textures is based on the ancient Taoist school of philosophy known as the *yin–yang* principle, which practically governs all aspects of Chinese life, and has been the guiding principle for all Chinese cooks. Consciously or unconsciously, every Chinese cook, from the housewife to the professional chef, works to the *yin–yang* principle, i.e. the harmonious balance and contrast in the conspicuous juxtaposition of different colours, aromas, flavours, shapes and textures, achieved by varying the ingredients, cutting techniques, seasonings and cooking methods.

The *yin-yang* symbol

Another characteristic of Chinese cuisine is the Chinese belief that all foods are also medicines – the overriding idea is that the kind of food one eats is closely relevant to one's health. This Taoist approach classifies all foods into those that possess the *yin*, meaning 'cool', quality, and those that possess the yang, or 'hot', quality. When the *yin–yang* forces in the body are not balanced, illness results. To combat this disorder, it is necessary to eat foods that will redress the balance. This belief was documented in the third century BC, at the inception of herbal medicine and the recognition of the link between nutrition and health, and it is still a dominant concept in Chinese culture today.

The *yin–yang* principle can also be seen in the basic dualism of nature: *yin* is feminine, dark, cool and passive; *yang*, in contrast, is masculine, bright, hot and active. But unlike the dualism of the Western world, in which good and evil are in perpetual conflict, *yin* and *yang* complement each other and form a harmonious pair, as symbolised by the interlocking figures within a perfect circle (above).

Over the years, as the *yin–yang* principle developed along dualist lines, it was combined with the 'five elements' concept of the Naturalism school of thought, which held that nature is made up of varying combinations of five elements of nature: metal, wood, water, fire and earth. The parallel to the four elements of the ancient Greeks – earth, fire, air and water – is striking.

The number five has always played an important part in Chinese food culture. Not only do we have the famous five-spice powder but we also have the five flavours seen as fundamental to Chinese cooking: sweet, sour, bitter, hot and salty. The earliest book on medicine, *Nei Jing* (Internal Channels), written over two thousand years ago, proposed that the body needed five flavours to live, five grains for nourishment, five fruits for support, five animals for benefit, and five vegetables for energy.

Regional cooking styles

China and its regions

China is a vast country, slightly smaller than Europe, but a little bigger than the United States of America. As can be expected, different regions enjoy different climates, natural resources and products. The variety of regional cooking styles and dishes is enormous, and the use of special condiments and cooking techniques results in different flavours even in similar ingredients.

In topographical outline, China is like a three-step West–East staircase. It starts in the West with the Tibetan plateau, 12,000 ft/4000 m above sea level. From the mountains on the eastern edge of this plateau, the land slopes away to highlands in Yunnan and Guizhou and the basins in Sichuan, mostly from 3000–6000 ft/1000–2000 m. It then descends further eastward to the hilly regions and plains below 100 ft/300 m on the middle and lower reaches of the Yangtze River.

Some areas in China are warm all the year round, while others have long winters and short summers. However most of the land lies in the temperate zone, with four distinct seasons. A combination of high temperature and plentiful rainfall provides favourable conditions for farming.

China has rich water resources. There are numerous lakes and rivers, and a coastline 8700 miles/14,000 km long, which touches on three seas of the Pacific Ocean – the Yellow Sea, the East China Sea and the South China Sea. A fourth sea, the Po Hai, is the western part of the Yellow Sea.

For centuries, the high mountains and deserts of the west and north and the seas and ocean to the east and south had protected China from invasion, but they have also isolated her from the rest of the world.

One interesting point to note here is that although a large variety of foodstuffs have been introduced into China since ancient times, these have all became integral ingredients of Chinese cuisine. The exception is milk and dairy products which, to this day have not taken a prominent place in the Chinese diet.

Looking at the map of China (on page xiii), it is not difficult to understand why there should be such a large diversity of cooking styles throughout the land. Yet, on closer inspection, you will be surprised to discover that there is hardly any difference in the fundamental principles of preparing and cooking the various foods in each region. From Beijing in the north to Guangdong (Canton) in the south, and from Sichuan in the west to Shanghai in the east, food is prepared, cooked and served according to the same rules and techniques passed down from generation to generation – whether from master chefs to their apprentices, or from home cooks to their offspring (usually mothers to daughters).

Traditionally, Chinese cuisine is divided into four main regional groups, as mentioned above (i.e. north, south, west and east), and within these groups, there are several cooking styles with subtle differences. Thus within the northern school, we have the renowned Shandong and Tianjin cuisine; then we have Yangzhou and Suzhou in Jiangsu and Hangzhou in Zheijiang, all loosely grouped under Shanghai cuisine; to the west we have Guizhou and Yunnan as well as Hunan (which is actually situated in the centre of China) closely associated with the hot and spicy Sichuan style of cooking; and in the south, besides Canton, we have Fujian and Taiwan, plus Hong Kong and Macau.

It is true to say that what distinguishes the various regional cooking is not so much the ingredients nor the cooking methods used, but the emphasis on condiments and seasonings used. For example, the northerners tend to use a lot of vinegar in their cooking, while easterners use more sugar, westerners like chillies and peppers, and southern food is supposed to have a greater amount of the 鮮 xian (delicious) flavouring, which is why Cantonese cooking is held in such high regard throughout China, and indeed all over the world.

The majority of the recipes in this book are Cantonese, although many other popular regional specialities such as Hot and Sour Soup, Shanghai 'Smoked' Fish, Sesame Prawn Toast, Bang Bang Chicken, Kung-Pao Chicken, Ma Po Tofu, and Aromatic Crispy Duck etc. are also included here for your enjoyment.

Serving of Chinese food

A certain uniqueness distinguishes Chinese cuisine from all other food cultures – perhaps with the exception of South-East Asia – not only in the preparation and cooking, but also in the serving and eating of the food. To start with, we do not follow the conventional Western serving sequence of soup, fish, meat, dessert course by course.

An informal Chinese meal

An informal Chinese meal is like a buffet, with all the different courses (including soup) placed in the centre of a round table for everyone to help themselves. Only at a formal dinner or banquet are the dishes served course by course, and even then the order of serving is not governed by the ingredients, but rather by the cooking methods, and dishes are seldom served individually (except items like Shark's Fin or Bird's Nest, etc.), but come in groups. For instance, the starters usually consist of cold cuts or/and deep-fried items. These should not be too strongly flavoured nor richly seasoned, and should always be dry or without any gravy. The main courses are usually rich and heavy with gravy or sauce to be served with plain rice, wheaten buns or pancakes. A light soup could be served between the starters and the main courses. Chinese soups are made from a chicken and meat stock, never too heavy. The popular Hot and Sour Soup or Sweetcorn and Chicken/Crabmeat Soup served in Chinese restaurants in the West are too heavy and filling, therefore should be avoided. As for Won Ton Soup, it is not really a soup but a dish to be eaten between meals as a snack. The same applies to fried rice and noodles – these should never be served with other dishes as part of the meal, but served on their own as a light luncheon or snack.

We never serve food on a plate to each person individually. A Chinese meal is served absolutely ready to eat – there is no last minute carving on the table, no dishing out separate items such as potatoes, vegetables, or gravy or other condiments. There is no long prelude when you all wait for everybody to be served before you start. At a Chinese table, when everyone is seated, the host will raise his chopsticks and say 'Chin, chin' (Please, please), and then you all pick up your chopsticks and enjoy yourselves.

The reason for serving Chinese food this way is partly because of the Chinese division between 飯 *fan* (grains such as rice, wheaten buns, dumplings and noodles, known as staples), and 菜 *cai* (pronounced choi or choy as in *bak choy*, which is meat, poultry, fish and vegetable dishes cooked in various ways, and known as supplementary food). It is in combining various ingredients and blending different flavours for the preparation of *cai* that demonstrates the fine art and skill of Chinese cuisine.

One cannot imagine Chinese food without rice, and the Chinese word for cooked rice, *fan*, is synonymous with food or a meal. It is so central to everyday Chinese life that when we greet friends, we ask them not how they are, but 'Have you eaten any *fan* yet?' Thus, the term 'rice bowl', besides being an eating utensil, has also become the symbol of livelihood – to have one's rice bowl broken means to have got the sack, and to possess an iron rice bowl means you have a job for life. Paradoxically, the expression *fan-tong* (a rice-bucket) means someone who can eat a lot of rice, but in reality is a good-for-nothing simpleton.

In China, an everyday meal must have a proper balance between *fan* and *cai*, which consists mostly of simply prepared and cooked dishes; while for a formal dinner or when dining out in restaurants, the balance is shifted to the *cai* dishes and the emphasis is on the presentation of these dishes, which can be very elaborate and lavish. No rice is served until the end of the meal as a token, for by then everyone is too full to want any 'staple' food. The exception is for a banquet to celebrate a wedding or a birthday, when both fried rice and noodles would be served (especially for a birthday party, because the Chinese regard the strips of noodles as symbolising a long life – hence the name 'longevity noodles').

What to drink with Chinese meals

Contrary to common belief, tea is seldom served at mealtimes in China. It is true that tea is the most popular beverage for most Chinese people, but it is usually drunk before or after a meal, not during.

Earlier, I mentioned the difference between *fan* and *cai* in Chinese food. *Cai* dishes are also divided into 酒菜 *jiu-cai* (wine dishes), food to be eaten with wine, or 飯菜 *fan-cai* (rice dishes), food to be eaten with rice or other grains.

'Wine dishes' are the cold starters, roasted and deep-fried dishes, as well as some stir-fried dishes. 'Rice dishes' are mostly braised and steamed dishes, as well as casseroles and dishes that contain a certain amount of gravy, including some of the stir-fried dishes.

In China, wine dishes are usually, but by no means always, served in restaurants rather than in homes, except on special occasions or when entertaining. For everyday lunches or suppers, rice dishes are usually served with a soup, not as a separate course, but throughout the meal.

I would also like to dispel the commonly held misconception that Chinese food and wine do not go well together. This is of course utter nonsense. Then there are those who recommend a white wine for *all* Chinese food. Obviously that cannot be right either, unless you happen to dislike drinking red wine. I believe all these misguided opinions are partly caused by the unconventional way the Chinese serve their food, which completely throws into confusion the Western convention (a rather tenuous one, in my humble opinion) of matching white wine with fish and white meat, and red wine with red meat, irrespective of how the dishes were cooked.

A Chinese meal is planned according to a carefully worked out programme based on the *yin–yang* principle – harmony and contrast. So we may have red meat before white meat or fish, but what determines the serving order of dishes or courses is not so much the ingredients, but rather the way they are prepared and cooked.

Choosing wine or wines for a Chinese meal should never be a big problem. The secret is not to try to match a particular wine with an individual dish but, rather, to look for a wine which will bring harmony to a course of different dishes, or be able to complete an overall equilibrium, since each Chinese dish or course of dishes is carefully balanced in accordance with the principle of a harmonious blending of colour, aroma, flavour and texture.

A bottle of Chinese wine

So the only point we have to observe here is that, as a rule, light wines (usually white or rosé, but also some reds) should be served before full-bodied and weighty wines (almost always red).

Although I am not a 'beer man', there is no reason why you should not drink beer or lager with Chinese food if you prefer beer to wine – many people in China do so.

After a good Chinese meal, nothing is more refreshing than a large pot of hot Chinese tea – without sugar or milk.

Deh-Ta Hsiung

Equipment and Techniques Used in a Chinese Kitchen

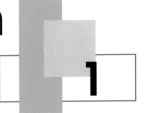

GENERAL EQUIPMENT

Wok range/burners

The wok range, the main source of heat for Chinese cooking, consists of short steel rings, used to support the round-bottomed woks, welded to a thick steel base plate. Underneath are the gas jet burners, which supply the fierce temperatures typical (and necessary) to produce authentic Chinese food. These gas jets (from 6–12), direct jets of burning gas towards a centrally placed, inverted, truncated cone, which directs the burning gas directly upwards to the base of the wok. Modern wok ranges tend to have the rings formed by pressing them directly from the base plate, thus producing a seamless one-piece construction. This has the added benefits of strength and resilience, as this method is less prone to cracking along the welds of ring/base plate as the traditional ranges were prone to.

On the top of these fixed rings are the actual wok supports. These are steel rings which sit inside the wok burner rings so that the woks are at the optimum height to benefit from the intense heat. These rings should be fitted so that the closed section is facing you and the open sections face off to the sides and away from you. This allows the excess heat to be vented away from your hands and body.

Another feature of the Chinese wok range is the constant flow of water that runs from the rear of the stove to the front, where there is a gully that leads to a drainage point. This has a dual purpose of keeping the stove cool and to prevent warping of the base plate due to the heat, and to wash any debris that may fall onto the base plate, keeping cleaning down to a minimum.

Wok ranges can be fitted with rear bar burners, so that stocks and hot water can be maintained and ready for use.

1

Steamers

All Chinese kitchens have a steamer of some description, as this method is a major part of Chinese cookery. These are usually multi part pieces of equipment that consist of: the main water reservoir, the steamer tray, and the lid. The use for each piece is self-explanatory. Larger kitchens would usually have a dedicated steaming unit, such as a dim sum steamer. These are large freestanding units, which can double up as a general purpose steamer, and are used to handle everything from fish and soups to shark's fin and abalone.

Most kitchens, however, use the combi oven. This piece of equipment combines the functions of an oven and a steamer.

Ovens/roasting oven

There are very few dishes in the Chinese culinary repertoire that use roasting as the main cooking method. The dishes which are known are synonymous with Chinese cooking (Peking duck, Char Siu, suckling pig, etc.).

Roasting in China is achieved by the method called 'hang roasting', using a roasting oven. Originally made of clay (nowadays steel), with an iron support rail along the upper inside edge to hang the ducks or meat from, these charcoal or wood-fired ovens roast to perfection. The heat generated is even and controlled via an adjustable vent in the lid.

Spit roasting is also used, mainly to handle large, single pieces of meat, such as whole roast belly of pork and suckling pigs. This method is commonly used by the wealthy/big restaurants, as it necessitates the building of a charcoal pit and spit.

In the West, Chinese chefs have to use the European style of oven which, although serviceable, are not high enough to recreate Chinese roasting styles, so most of the time the meat/poultry is overdone (as in order to achieve an even colour, turning is required, which increases the cooking times). With the introduction of the combi oven, this matter has been overcome, as the new ovens are high enough to accommodate whole hanging ducks and strips of meat.

Woks

These large bowl-shaped pans are the icon of Chinese cookery. Their rounded shape promotes even conduction of heat and the thinness of the metal allows for rapid heating and maintenance of that heat. Their shape also allows the wok to be safely set upon the wok burners without fear of rolling and spilling the contents.

Traditional woks had two small metal handles that were fixed to either side of the main bowl of the wok. This meant that you had to handle the wok with a thick cloth and tossing the food required both strength and skill.

Most woks available these days have a metal socket, to which a wooden handle is attached. This makes handling the wok less hazardous.

A contemporary wok

Ideally, the wok should be made from mild steel, that is, steel that has a high carbon content and is fairly soft (in steel terms). This means that the wok will react with acids and rust easily if not maintained properly (see Seasoning and cleaning a new wok, page 12). Stainless steel is not a suitable material as it does not conduct heat as easily and cannot be seasoned properly for Chinese cooking. The best size of wok to begin with would be 12 inches (30cm) in diameter. This size will easily handle up to two main course portions, or one noodle dish portion (using the stated quantities for the recipes in this book). The next size up and the one that should become the standard wok size for general kitchen use is the 14 inch (35cm) diameter wok. This size wok can easily handle up to four main course size portions, or two noodle dish portions.

Large domed lids, of the appropriate size, are also available for the woks. These are used when the wok is to be used for steaming, braising or stewing.

Wok ladles

These are effectively a shallow metal bowl attached to a handle. They are made from stainless steel to facilitate cleaning. The ladles come in two sizes, which are determined by the capacity/volume of the bowl. The standard size ladle is approximately 10fl oz, and the smaller one is 5fl oz. The standard size is used for portion control and dispenses with any need for measuring jugs and scales, as once you become accustomed to using the wok ladle, you can determine how much of an ingredient you are using by how much there is in the ladle.

The standard size ladle is also used to add seasonings to a dish being cooked. This requires experience and judgement, as you can easily over season if you are not careful. The smaller ladle is mainly used to dispense sauces into dishes that are being cooked.

The ladle is the main utensil used for stir-frying. Its shape may perplex some into wondering how such a strange shaped utensil is used in such a fast cooking method, as it looks quite heavy and clumsy, but you have to actually use it to see its benefits. Your first couple of tries will undoubtedly be difficult, but perseverance will result in understanding, and you will then be able to handle any type of technique that requires the use of a wok and wok ladle.

The wok ladle is also used to help toss the food in the wok so that the food items are cooked evenly. (See Tossing food in a wok, page 12.)

Wok spatula

A wok spatula

This utensil is the one which will be most familiar to anyone who has done stir-frying before. It is essentially a Chinese fish slice, without the perforations. It is used mainly for turning shallow-fried items, and for cooking dishes using the 'raw stir-frying' or 'exploding oil (you bao)' techniques, where speed is of the essence. It can also be used for stir-frying but you will find that because of its flat shape, you will be unable to toss food in the wok. Useful for beginners.

Chinese cleavers (knives)

Chinese chefs use what are generically called cleavers for the preparation of meat, fish, poultry and vegetables. The Chinese character for cleaver literally translates into 'knife', so the word cleaver is in fact a misnomer. I suppose they are called cleavers because they resemble European cleavers in appearance. Chinese knives are split into two types, No 1 and No 2.

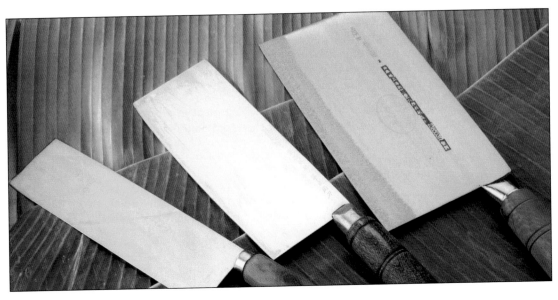

A selection of Chinese cleavers

The No 1 knife (blade) is around $8-8\frac{1}{2}$ inches (21–22cm) long and around $4-4\frac{1}{2}$ inches (10–11cm) wide. The blade edge should be very slightly curved and not flat. The knives can be made from either carbon steel or stainless steel. Carbon steel is softer and can be honed to a fine edge, but reacts badly to acids and poor maintenance (can chip easily and needs to be regularly sharpened). Stainless steel is acid resistant and much harder, it holds its edge for longer but can be difficult to re-sharpen to its original edge. These knives are available as all metal, or metal blade and wooden handle. Whichever type you choose, it should feel balanced in your hand.

Cleavers come in two thicknesses. The thin-bladed version is generally used for cutting meat, poultry, fish and vegetables into small pieces for cooking. The thicker-bladed (and correspondingly heavier) version is used for heavy work, where cutting through bones is required.

The smaller No 2 knife is about 8 inches (20cm) long and 3 inches (8cm) wide and is generally used to prepare vegetables and in situations where using the No 1 knife is impractical. There are also versions of this knife with a $\frac{3}{4}-1\frac{1}{4}$ inch (2–3cm) blade which are used to carve the skin off Peking duck in front of customers.

Other knives available but very rarely seen are the large butcher's cleavers, which are around twice the width and length of a No 1 cleaver, with the front half of the blade curving to the tip of the knife.

Skimmers and spiders

These are invaluable in the Chinese kitchen for removing food items from water or oil. The spider is a wire 'web' attached to a long handle. Chinese versions have a handle of bamboo with a brass wire 'web', while

European versions are made wholly of stainless steel. The skimmer is similar to the spider, the only difference is that the head of the skimmer is made of a fine metal mesh. Skimmers are used to skim oil after deep frying food, to remove any fine particles of food that a spider might not pick up, due to its large mesh size.

A spider is used when blanching meat in oil or vegetables in water. Its large mesh size allows for the rapid draining of oil or water.

Colanders

These are large stainless steel bowls with many holes, two handles and a foot and are used for draining large quantities of food after boiling or blanching.

Chopping boards

A traditional chopping board

Traditional Chinese chopping boards were usually a large piece of tree trunk, around 4–8 inches (10–20cm) thick and anything up to 18 inches (45cm) in diameter. These are still available in the UK, but tend to crack once wet, as they are made from young wood that has not been aged and dried properly. They used to come bound with metal straps around the circumference to prevent the cracking, but these became dirt traps and their use was discontinued. Modern pressure-treated hardwood chopping boards and heavy duty polythene chopping boards are a much more hygienic and reliable alternative.

Bamboo steamers

A bamboo steamer

These steamers are wholly constructed from bamboo, and make an excellent container for steaming food. The base is made from strips of bamboo held together with twine made from thin strips of bamboo. There are gaps between each of the strips, which allow steam to pass upwards and over the food. The sides are made from large strips of bamboo that have been soaked in water and wound round to form a ring to which the base is attached. The lid is also bamboo. This material is ideal for steaming as it allows steam to pass through its structure, cooking the food, without condensing on the inner surfaces and dripping back down onto the food, diluting its flavour.

Bamboo steamers are available in many sizes, from 4 inches (10cm) to 18 inches (45cm) in diameter.

Sandpot, Claypot

This is a traditional Chinese casserole dish used for braising and stewing. It is made from a sand-coloured clay which has been glazed on the inner surface only. The outer surface is bound with metal wire. The short handle is hollow and also made from the same sand-coloured clay, as is the lid. The lid is glazed on the outer surface not the inner, and is usually pierced with a small hole to allow steam to escape. Very brittle and easily broken, these pots need to be soaked in water before first use to prevent cracking, although if started on a low heat, this can be prevented. Modern versions are made from aluminium or stainless steel.

GENERAL TECHNIQUES

How to hold and cut with a Chinese cleaver

The Chinese cleaver is an extremely versatile knife and, correctly handled, it becomes a multi-purpose tool in the preparation of ingredients in the kitchen.

The correct way to hold a Chinese cleaver is to grip the handle and brace the blade using your forefinger and thumb, much the same way as you hold a standard European cook's knife. Because of the weight and depth of the blade, it may feel slightly unwieldy at first, but once you become accustomed to the feel of the cleaver, you will wonder how you managed to do without one for so long!

When using the Chinese cleaver to cut food, it is best to guide the blade using the first joints of your fore and middle fingers as a guide rail against the blade. This will ensure that the food will be cut to a uniform thickness.

The blade should never be raised higher than the first joint of the forefinger, as this will greatly increase the chance of an injury, due to the loss of guidance of the blade from the finger.

Cutting techniques

There are many cutting techniques employed in the Chinese kitchen in the preparation of raw food. Below are some of the most commonly used techniques, ones that are used in this book.

Slicing

There are many ways of slicing in the Chinese culinary repertoire. The standard techniques are:

Push slice This method is the standard way for cutting all meat and poultry. The blade, using the first and middle finger joints as a guide,

should be pushed firmly forwards and downwards (tip to heel) in one swift motion. The slices of meat cut from the pieces should be around 1mm thick. The way to tell if you have performed this technique correctly is the thickness of the slice, and whether or not there are any knife marks on the surface of the meat. Knife marks mean that there was 'sawing' of the meat, i.e. the meat was not cut in one go.

Pull slice This method is used to cut slices from thin pieces of meat such as chops, fish fillets and poultry breasts. The blade is held at an angle of 25–30 degrees from the horizontal surface of the item. The item is braced with your fingers at the end from which the first slice is to be taken, and the blade is drawn from the heel to the tip towards yourself, much like slicing an escalope.

Butterfly cut (slice), double pull slice This method is used to cut fish fillets for poaching: Completing the first cut, the skin of the fish fillet is not cut through, it is only on the second cut that it is severed completely. This results in two slices of fish held together by a thin piece of skin.

When cooked, the skin curls and contracts and pulls the flesh of the fish around itself. This results in a shape reminiscent of a butterfly, hence the name, butterfly cut.

Horizontal slicing This method is use to cut large thin slices from thin pieces of meat and poultry before cutting it into shreds. This is possibly the most dangerous method, so extreme care must be taken.

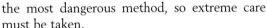

The meat or poultry is placed onto the chopping board and a hand is placed flat on top to prevent any movement. The cleaver is then held parallel to the chopping board, 2–3mm above, and the blade is drawn from heel to tip along the piece of meat slowly and in one motion (if possible).

Chopping

Lock chopping This method is used to cut through meat, such as ribs, or whole poultry. The meat or poultry is cut down to the bone, then, with the heel of the cleaver in contact with the bone, the cleaver and item are brought up together and slammed down onto the chopping board, the momentum helping to cut through the bone. Only to be used on raw meat and poultry, never cooked, as this would pulverise the item.

Double blade chopping This method is the Chinese way of mincing. The meat or poultry is first cut up into small pieces to aid the process. Then, with a cleaver in each hand, the meat or poultry is chopped, starting from one end and working across to the other. The meat or poultry is then folded into half and then half again, using the cleavers as spatulas. The chopping process is then repeated until the desired texture is achieved.

Crushing and mincing of garlic and ginger

This is one of the standard ways of preparing garlic and ginger for Chinese dishes. The 'root' end of the garlic cloves are removed, and one

by one, each clove is hit hard with the flat side of the cleaver. This has the effect of causing the skin to separate from the flesh and is then easily removed. The garlic flesh is then chopped to the required size.

Ginger is usually scraped free of skin using the cleaver. The ginger is then cut into rounds 3–4 mm thick. As with garlic, each round is struck soundly with the flat side of the cleaver, and the resulting mass chopped finely to cut up any fibres.

Slices

Beef, lamb and pork should be cut into long strips with a 'face' or cross section of $1\frac{1}{4}$ inch (30mm) (h) × $2\frac{1}{2}$ inch (60mm) (w). The resulting slices should be cut 1mm thick.

Chicken and duck breasts, because of their awkward shape, are best cut using the pull slice method. The resulting slices will need to be trimmed to neaten their appearance. Poultry slices can be up to 3mm thick.

Shredding

Beef, lamb and pork should be sliced using the push slicing or horizontal slicing methods to give 2mm thick slices. These slices should then be cut into strips of approximately 60mm (l) × 2mm (h) × 2mm (w).

Chicken and duck breasts should be cut into slices using the horizontal slicing method and then cut into strips of the same dimensions as above.

Beef fillet and pork fillet should not be shredded, as their soft nature will cause them to fall apart during the cooking process if they are cut this fine.

Strips

These are meat or poultry cut into 5mm thick slices and then into the following size: 60mm (l) × 5mm (h) × 5mm (w). Beef steak (sirloin, fillet) and pork fillet are suitable for this, as are chicken breast and fillets of firm white fish. Other cuts of beef, pork and duck breast would be unsuitable as they would result in an extremely chewy dish.

Cubes/dice

Beef and lamb should first be cut into slices 25mm thick, then again into strips 1 inch (25mm) wide and finally into cubes 1 inch (25mm) (l) × 1 inch (25mm) (h) × 1 inch (25mm) (w).

This cut is used for stews and braised dishes. For stir-frying, 5mm dice is recommended.

For chicken, the same procedure should be followed, but the dimensions should be 15mm (l) × 15mm (h) × 15mm (w).

Cutting up a fresh lobster

First turn the lobster over on its back so its belly is facing upwards. Using a strong knife, cut all the way along the length of the lobster where its legs meet. This will cut through all its main nerve centres and kill it almost instantly (this must be done within 10 seconds). The lobster may thrash around when it is turned over, so extreme care must be taken when doing this.

Then cut the head away from the tail, and detach the claws from the head. Pull the legs away from the head and remove the gills, then cut away the mouthparts and the tips of the legs. Remove the stomach sac from the head. Place any light green tomalley (liver) and dark green coral (roe) into a separate bowl.

Split the tail of the lobster down the middle, remove the intestinal tract, and cut each half into 3–4 pieces, depending on size. Cut the claws away from the 'knuckle'. Using the flat side of a cleaver, crack the knuckles and the claw shells so that when cooked, the meat will be easily accessed.

Cutting up a fresh crab

Using a strong brush, scrub the crab under a stream of running water to remove any mud and sand. The crab may get active at this point, so care must be taken to be aware of where the claws are. On a chopping board place the crab on its back, and using a dinner knife prise open the 'purse', the flap on its under side. The crab will not like this and will become *very* agitated. Using a strong skewer, pierce the small exposed dimple and push all the way down to the back, in and out several times. This will destroy the major nerve centre of the crab and kill it. The crab will become floppy at this point.

Remove the 'purse' and, using a strong knife, cut along the line exposed between the legs. Grab the legs on one side and pull sharply to remove from the carapace. Repeat on the other side. Remove the gills and claws from each half, and cut off the tips of the legs. Using a meat bat, crack the shell on the legs and claws.

Remove the stomach sac from the head of the crab. Feel inside the head and remove the clear film from either side of the head. Using a meat bat, gently tap along the natural line on the edge of the carapace to remove the excess shell. Drain off any liquid that collects in the head.

THE WOK

Seasoning and cleaning a new wok

When you have purchased your first wok, you need to clean and season it before use. Most modern woks are made by pressing a sheet of mild steel into the required shape, then trimming back the edges and finally riveting on the handle. This process uses machine oil to facilitate release of the metal from the die, and this has to be cleaned off before the wok can be used.

First hot water and detergent should be used to remove the oil from the wok, followed by a hot water rinse. The wok should be dried, then placed onto the stove and strongly heated until the entire surface has become a dark grey colour. There will be a lot of smoke at this stage, as any remaining oil that is impregnated into the surface of the metal is burnt off. If any of the darkened surfaces are shiny, that area needs to be reheated until it becomes white and ashen, as the shiny areas will be partially unoxidised machine oil. Needless to say, efficient extraction is vital to prevent choking on the fumes and smoke.

The wok should be allowed to cool, wiped down to remove any ashes, then gently heated. Some fresh cooking oil should be applied to the wok using clean kitchen paper. The wok should be wiped down in a circular manner and the oil and paper regularly changed until there is no trace of carbon/black matter left on the paper.

The wok is now ready for use. After every use, the wok should be cleaned only using hot water and a metal pan scrubber. Detergent should not be used on a seasoned wok. If there is a major build-up of burnt food on the wok, it should be cleaned by strong heating on the wok stove till all deposits become carbonised and then white ash. This should then be wiped off and the wok re-seasoned following the above method.

Woks should never be used for acidic foods and sauces, as these will strip off the seasoning that will have built up, which helps to prevent any food from sticking to the wok.

Tossing food in a wok

This technique allows a chef, while stir-frying, to move food about in a hot wok without it catching and burning. It also allows the small pieces of food to be rapidly and evenly cooked. This technique is facilitated by the curved shape of the wok, the use of the wok ladle, and the wok stove. The wok is quickly pulled back towards yourself, the edge of the wok ring is used to relieve the weight of the wok and its contents; at the same time, the wok ladle is used to push the food forward, and the front of the wok brought up sharply to help turn the food back to the centre of the wok. Care needs to be taken at this point, as too much strength used in the push will cause all the food to fly out the opposite side of the wok, or if the return is too strong, the food will miss the centre of the wok and fall onto your hands. The wok should then be allowed to fall back to its natural position on the wok stove. With practice, you will be able to perform this five or six times in a row before needing to rest your arm. The movement is essentially the opposite of tossing food in a sauté pan in the European manner.

Cooking techniques using a wok

'Running/passing' through oil 走油 (Zou You)

This technique is basically blanching marinated meat, poultry, fish or shellfish in hot oil to partially cook it before finishing off in the wok as a stir-fry. It is this technique of part cooking the meat portion of the dish that enables stir fries to be so quick to produce.

The procedure is to fill a wok one third to one half full of oil, and strongly heat until it is very hot but not smoking (around 180–190° C). An oil thermometer can be used to determine this temperature, but generally, when the oil has become water-like in its consistency, it is close to the required temperature. Another way to test the temperature is to add a few coriander leaves to the oil; if they immediately pop and crisp up, then the oil is ready. At this point turn off the heat and add the marinated meat, using a wok ladle, then quickly stir the meat to separate and prevent the pieces from sticking together.

As soon as the meat changes colour, turn the heat back up to maximum and continue stirring for 30 seconds. Turn off the heat and quickly remove all the blanched meat to a colander using an appropriate-sized spider. The meat should be half cooked at this stage and have a silky, smooth feel when touched. This is due to the potato starch used in the marinade, and is what gives the meat a silky/velvet texture in the mouth. The meat should not be overcooked and dry, nor should it have a brown crusty exterior. If it is, the finished dish will be dry and hard to eat.

If the oil is too hot, the potato starch in the marinade will instantly cook and stick all the meat together in a great mass and brown too quickly. If this happens it will be necessary to separate the mass, which will cause some of the meat to tear and will result in uncooked/blanched meat in the centre, which will require additional cooking before use. It will also result in the untidy appearance of the finished dish.

If the oil is not hot enough, the meat will just sit and absorb oil. This is easily corrected by removing the meat from the oil, and reheating the oil to the required temperature.

Care must taken when using this technique, as it involves heating a large quantity of oil using a powerful heat source to high temperatures without the security of a thermostat. The oil must never be left unattended while heating on a wok stove, as it will reach its flashpoint in a faster time than if it were heated on a conventional stove.

Stir-frying 炒 (Chow/Chao)

This is the method of cooking that is synonymous with Chinese cookery. It is the main cooking technique used all over China. The skill of stir-frying is at its highest in Southern China, especially Guangdong (formerly Canton).

The most essential part of stir-frying is a well seasoned wok and a fierce heat source. Some would also say the freshest and best quality ingredients, and I do not disagree with this, but first class ingredients are useless if they are to be cooked using equipment and heat that is not up to the required standard.

The wok needs to be heated, without oil, until it begins to smoke. A small amount of oil is then added and the cooking can begin immediately. Oil should not be added to the wok before the wok is heated as although the oil will be at the right temperature, the metal will not be hot enough to maintain a reasonable temperature once the food ingredients are added to it.

The oil used should be of neutral taste and smell, such as peanut, sunflower, vegetable, etc. Sesame oil should not be used as a cooking oil, as it easily scorches and burns and will leave an overpowering taste in the finished dish. Olive oil of any sort should not be used, since this oil is not native to Chinese cooking, therefore it will leave the finished dish with an odd taste.

When stir-frying, it is essential to have all ingredients, prepared and marinated, on a tray ready to hand to be added to the wok in turn. As mentioned previously, the wok needs to be heated till smoking, before the oil is added. Any aromatics required for the dish (ginger or garlic) are added at this point and stirred quickly to release their aromas before the other ingredients are added in turn (in order of required cooking times) to the wok. The food items need to be constantly moved and tossed to ensure even cooking and to prevent burning due to the intense heat. The seasonings and sauces will generally be arrayed on a shelf in front of the chef, where they can be added using the wok ladle.

Caution must be used when adding seasoning to a dish using a wok ladle, as the ladle will tend to pick up more seasoning than is required because it will be damp from oil or food juices. It is best to add a little seasoning at a time, then taste and correct the seasoning. Because of the intense heat source used you can actually turn the heat down to low, add the seasoning, and then turn the heat back up to maximum, thicken if required with potato starch and water paste, before finishing with a little sesame oil and white pepper, before dishing up.

Control of the heat source from the wok stove is the mark of a good Chinese chef. Knowing how much heat is required to cook a dish to perfection is a skill that can only be achieved from years of practice. Most stir-fried dishes require the strongest heat possible to give the food a 'wok aroma', an essence of Chinese cookery that cannot be obtained elsewhere and is characteristic of a stir-fry. Many dishes (and the skills of the chef) are assessed by the amount of 'wok aroma' they possess. Not all dishes require the strongest heat setting; green leafy vegetables cooked at this temperature will no doubt have 'wok aroma', but they will also be scorched and dry.

The various cooking methods that use the wok are listed below, along with descriptions of how to control the heat to obtain the best results.

'Raw' stir-frying 生炒 (Sang Chow/Sheng Chao)

This method is basically stir-frying a meat/poultry/fish/shellfish dish from its raw marinated state to the finished dish. This method differs from 'traditional' stir-frying in that the main ingredient (meat/poultry/fish/shellfish) has not been partially pre-cooked by 'running through oil'. It goes in raw and comes out cooked.

The wok is first heated on a high heat until smoking, a small amount of oil is added and swirled round to coat the wok. The main ingredient is then added and quickly separated out using a wok spatula, not a wok ladle, as you need to be able to turn the food constantly and not toss it. This rapid scooping and turning prevents any sticking and burning. It also prevents the food from browning – a characteristic of most 'raw' stir-fried dishes is a silky smooth finish to the main ingredient and good wok aroma. Any additional ingredients are added at various stages, depending on the degree of cooking required, and if it gets too dry, wine or stock can be added to provide some moisture. Thickening is rarely required as very little juice or liquid is produced, and those are usually bound up by the potato starch used in the marinade.

Deep-frying 炸 (Ja/Zha)

This method is the same as its European counterpart, except that it is slightly more dangerous. A wok is half filled with oil and strongly heated to a high temperature (190–200° C). Use a thermometer for this. Control of the temperature is vitally important, as deep-fried food should be dry and crisp, not soft and oil laden. The food items are usually quite thin, coated and chilled before being added to the oil. This chilling before cooking will prevent the food from cooking too quickly and also limits the amount of 'curling' that occurs when deep-frying, especially with prawns. Having a spider to hand also helps, because as soon as you can see the food browning too quickly, it can be removed immediately. In Chinese deep-frying, the food items generally require frying twice. The first time is to cook the food through; when the food item is removed from the oil to drain, it will generate steam from within, which will soften the crisp outside coating, thus necessitating the second frying. The purpose of the second frying is to crisp the outside coating. This second frying needs to be done at a much higher temperature (220° C) for a brief amount of time, as you only need to crisp the outside without cooking the inside any further.

If the oil becomes too hot and is browning the food too fast without thorough cooking, the best way to bring down the temperature to the desired level is to ladle in some cool oil. You also need to remove any excess oil from the wok (back to the halfway mark) once the appropriate temperature is achieved. This is to avoid overflowing.

'Exploding' oil method 油爆 (You Bao)

This is an advanced method that should be tried only once standard stir-frying and 'going through oil' have been mastered. The name of the method is a literal translation of what happens, but with a little care, major (and minor) oil burns can be avoided. This method is primarily used to cook (fully or partially) fish and shellfish (prawns, cephalopods, molluscs) in preparation for further stir frying, or for immediate use in cold salads or starters.

The wok is filled to about one-third full with oil, which is then strongly heated till it is very nearly smoking. The chilled raw food items – marinated (no potato starch) or unmarinated – are carefully added to the hot oil and separated with either a wok ladle or spatula. Great care must be taken at this point as the reaction of the wet, cold food when it comes into contact with the hot oil will be very vigorous – this is when 'exploding' (and most injuries) occur. If the food items are not marinated, then it is an easy matter to separate the individual pieces, but if they have been lightly marinated, you need to work very fast with the spatula or ladle to prevent the food items from catching. The food items should be removed from the oil and allowed to drain when they are slightly underdone; they will continue to cook when removed from the oil. It is very important that the food is not overcooked and dry, as the whole purpose of this technique is to maintain a juicy succulence to the food.

A safer way to use this method is to use a spider dipped in oil, on which the food items are laid out. The food is then basted with the boiling oil, and periodically moved to prevent sticking, until the required level of cooking is achieved. This method has the advantage of precise control of the cooking time and no drying out of the ingredient.

A famous dish cooked using this method is crystal shrimps.

Poaching 浸 (Jum/Jin)

This is the same as its European counterpart. The Chinese character for poaching means 'to soak', and is used to describe the method for cooking in liquid. The first method is the most simple, it is used to gently cook very fresh fish and top quality poultry or pork, so that its own taste shines through. A very large pot or wok, deep enough to comfortably hold the item, is two-thirds filled with water or plain unseasoned stock and brought to the boil, then the heat is turned down to a barely perceptible simmer. In its simplest form, the food is cooked and then served, dressed with soy sauce, hot oil and shredded spring onions (if fish) or various accompaniments (chicken or pork). Pork and poultry cooked in this way are known as 'white cut' pork or chicken, a reference to the cooking method.

The second way is exactly the same as the above method, except that the water or stock is seasoned, and infused with ginger and spring onions in order to counter any rank odours. The meat, poultry or fish is then finished in the same manner as above.

Control of the heat while poaching is very important. If the liquid is allowed to boil for any length of time, the food item will toughen up (meat and poultry) or break up (fish). The aim is to cook the food item without disturbing it.

Steaming 蒸 (Zheng)

This is one of the oldest methods of cookery used in the Chinese kitchen. Its most basic form is a covered bamboo basket, supported by bamboo chopsticks or rack, above a wok of boiling water, which is then covered with a wok lid. It is impractical to steam in a wok that is available on the market (13–15 inch (32–36cm) diameter) as they are too small to steam anything larger than a 1lb (454g) fish. It is much easier to buy a larger multi-stack steamer from a Chinese grocer/catering supplier.

Chinese cookery involves steaming marinated pork and beef, something that is very rarely seen in European cookery. The dish is usually flavoured with various types of preserved or fermented vegetable, in order to liven up the plain, simple taste of the steamed meat.

Fish and shellfish are also popular candidates for steaming, as this method maintains their delicate texture and fresh flavour. The steaming of fish and shellfish is called 'plain' steaming, a reference to the basic no frills method of cookery. The various regions of China have their own steamed dishes particular to that area.

Stewing 燜 (Mun/Men)

This method is the same as its European counterpart, in that food is cooked in a wok or pot over a low, direct flame. This method is particularly useful for tough cuts of meat that need tenderising through long slow cooking (beef brisket, pork knuckle). Care needs to be taken if this method is to be used in a wok on a wok stove, as it is very easy for the meat to catch on the bottom. This method is used mainly to cook exotic Chinese seafoods, such as abalone and sea cucumber.

Braising 炖 (Dun)

This method is not the same as European braising as the Chinese do not cook food in covered ceramic/metallic containers in the oven. The oven is used for roasting and even then it is, in appearance, nothing like its European cousin.

Chinese braising is a term used to describe cooking food in covered containers either by steaming or sitting, supported, in boiling water, till it is meltingly tender, so it is really a form of double boiling. There are two different methods in the preparation of the ingredients for braising.

The first involves part cooking the meat, and then combining it with various sauces and vegetables and then braising. Only a small amount of sauce or liquid is used, so that the cooking juices combine with the sauce to form a concentrated liquor. The second method is similar to the first, but a lot more sauce/stock is used to cover all the ingredients before it is braised. The resulting liquor is then drained off, seasoned and thickened before being returned to the dish. Dried scallops are cooked in this way for Chinese New Year and banquets.

Red braising 红烧 (Hong Shao)

This method of cookery is in fact stewing rather than braising, and confusingly, the literal Chinese translation is 'red roasting', a reference to the colour of the finished dish which looks roasted. It is a method of cookery popular in the northern reaches of China. It is usually made with pork that has been fried, on a high heat, to a light golden brown, and then cooked in stock that has been flavoured with yellow rock sugar, star anise, cassia, tangerine peel and Shao Xing wine. The deep red brown colour is obtained from the addition of dark soy sauce. The pork is cooked at a low simmer till tender, at which point the heat is turned up and the liquid reduced to a thick savoury caramel.

Roasting 烤, 烧 (Kao or Shao)

The Chinese method of roasting differs from the European method in the way the meat is hung while roasting and the fact that all meat for roasting has been marinated.

The Chinese oven is like a huge chimney; it is essentially a metal cylindrical tube on legs, with an upturned lip at the bottom to catch any oil drips. Near the top of the oven is a rail from which to hang the meat or poultry for roasting. On top of this goes the lid, into which is set the temperature regulator, a piece of metal over a hole in the lid. The degree of heat is regulated by how open the hole is: fully open is cool, fully closed is the hottest setting. The heat source is a double banjo burner, with a regulator as a safety measure.

Control of heat when cooking on a wok burner

The control of the intensity of the gas flame when using a wok burner to stir-fry, braise, stew, or deep-fry food, is vitally important. Knowing when to use a high heat and when to use a medium or low heat to produce a perfectly cooked dish is something that comes with experience, but if you follow the steps opposite, you will be on your way to becoming a competent wok chef.

Controlling the heat on a wok burner

1. What type of dish are you going to be cooking?

   A stir-fried dish requires high temperatures and a quick hand. A stewed or braised dish will require the lowest setting possible to maintain a gentle simmer. Deep-frying will require a high temperature and a watchful eye.

2. Are the main ingredients soft in texture or firm?

   Soft ingredients will require gentler handling and a medium heat. Firm ingredients can be tossed and subjected to higher temperatures.

3. Does the dish contain too much liquid?

   If so, a high heat is required to reduce the liquid down as fast as possible, without overcooking the ingredients. An alternative is to remove the excess liquid with a wok ladle.

How to stir-fry if you do not have a wok range/burners

Although wok burners are becoming more widely available, it is still a major undertaking to fit one into an existing kitchen, unless it is a small single burner type.

Solid tops are the most common type of cooking range to be found in the kitchen and these can produce good results. The rings on the solid top can be pulled out, and the wok sat into the hole, directly over the flame. This will get the wok nice and hot, ready to cook, but there will not be the precise control over the heat that you can achieve with a wok burner. Tossing food in the wok on a solid top is problematical to say the least,

as a solid top is about 10cm higher than a wok range, and the wok sits in a depression rather than on a support ring, therefore it takes more effort to toss the food.

Flat-bottomed woks can be used, but these are designed for use on domestic electric or gas hobs and not solid tops. They would not conduct heat very well if sat directly onto the solid top, as the diameter of the flat base is very small.

One way around this is to use a pot on the solid top to produce the stir-fry. I would recommend using a thin aluminium pot (2mm thick sides and bottom) of 10 inch (25cm) diameter. This can be placed onto the solid top (or open ring gas burner) and heated, without any oil, until smoking. Oil can be added at this point, and the ingredients (par-cooked meat or poultry and raw vegetables) to be cooked added immediately. Steam can then be generated by the addition of small amounts of wine and/or stock, taking care not to add too much so that the temperature drops and the food begins to boil. The dish can then be finished off as per the recipe.

This method works best on an open ring gas burner.

Basic Ingredients in a Chinese Kitchen

2

Salt The most commonly used condiment in any kitchen. Used in conjunction with sugar and white pepper to balance the flavour of a dish.

White pepper (ground) Used at the end of the cooking of a dish to add fragrance and a touch of heat. Also used in meat marinades (along with ginger, spring onion and wine) to counteract any strong (rank) odours.

Black pepper Very rarely used in Chinese cooking, as the pungency and perfume of black pepper tends to overwhelm the flavours in most dishes.

Yellow rock sugar This sugar is partially refined and retains quite a lot of its natural flavour. It comes in large yellow lumps that require breaking apart into manageable pieces before use. Mainly used in some stews and braised dishes to add a touch of sweetness. Also used in sweet soups.

Slice sugar This type of sugar consists of a layer of light brown sugar pressed between two layers of brown sugar. Used in sweet soups and also in some stews and braised dishes.

Rice vinegar; Seasoned soy sauce; Oyster sauce; Dark soy sauce

Sesame oil (roasted) Made from grinding and pressing roasted sesame seeds. Can be made from black or white sesame seeds. Only used at the end of a dish to add fragrance. Not to be used as the primary cooking oil as the flavour would overpower everything else.

Soy sauce (light) Made from fermenting steamed soy beans, salt and barley flour, this seasoning is synonymous with Chinese cooking. Should only be used to flavour dishes, not as a primary seasoning agent.

Soy sauce (dark) Traditionally, this was the by-product of soy sauce production. The light soy sauce would be drained away and the heavier sediment that remained was either re-fermented or used as dark soy sauce. Nowadays, lower grade or second ferment soy sauce is mixed with caramel to form dark soy sauce. Like gravy browning, this ingredient is used mainly to colour dishes to the required depth, as there is no tradition of using reduced brown stocks in Chinese cookery.

Oyster sauce This rich brown flavouring sauce is made from a reduction of oysters, water, sugar, salt and spices. It has a rich savoury/sweet flavour and goes well with all meat, poultry, fish, shellfish and vegetables. Mainly used in southern China. Some detractors of southern Chinese cuisine say that without oyster sauce, it (southern cuisine) would not be as famous as it is.

Red vinegar A unique tasting vinegar from the Shanghai (eastern) region of China. Mainly

Red vinegar

Chinkiang vinegar

used as a dipping sauce for steamed shellfish and a condiment for soups, most notably shark's fin and hot and sour.

Chinkiang vinegar This thick dark aromatic vinegar from south-eastern China has a subtly smoky sweet flavour. Used as a dipping sauce for dumplings, in marinades and stir frying. Has been referred to as the balsamic vinegar of the East. A main component of the original sweet and sour dishes.

White rice vinegar Made and used in all parts of China. Mainly used in pickling vegetables.

Hoisin sauce Traditionally made from the remains of soy sauce production, the soy bean pulp is recooked with garlic, chillies and a variety of seasonings to produce this thick dark brown/purple savoury sweet sauce. Used in marinades, stir frying of red meats, and most commonly as the sauce accompaniment for Peking and aromatic crispy duck.

Yellow bean sauce (crushed) This thick dark brown sauce is a northern Chinese ingredient, mainly used in stews and braises. Also used in marinades and some stir fries.

Shao Xing wine This wine from eastern China is made from cereals. It has a sherry-like fragrance and amber colour. Mainly used in stir-fried dishes to add fragrance and in marinades to counter 腥 strong odours (*xing*). Also used in some 'drunken' dishes.

Shao Xing wine (Hua Diao) This is the same wine as above, but of a much higher quality. Where most Shao xing wine is mass produced, *Hua Diao* is made using traditional methods, hence the price is usually four to five times that of normal Shao xing.

Rose liqueur (Mei Kuei Lu Chiew) This is Kao Liang (a distilled spirit) that has rose petals infused into it prior to the distillation. It has a strong smell of roses and is quite sweet. Used in marinades of red meats and some drunken dishes. Must be used sparingly otherwise it will overpower the dish.

Chilli oil 1 (also known as 'red oil') Made by steeping dried red chilli flakes in hot oil. How hot the oil becomes depends on the type of chilli flakes used. Used to flavour Sichuan dishes.

Chilli oil 2 This chilli oil is made from slow-cooking fresh red chillies, garlic, shallots and dried shrimps in oil until nearly all the moisture is removed. When cool, the mixture is stirred up and equal amounts of oil and sediment is served. Mainly used as a dipping sauce.

Chilli sauce This is made from ground salted red chillies and white rice vinegar. Used as a dipping sauce.

Hot bean sauce Made from fermented broad beans, chilli, garlic and various seasonings. Comes in varying degrees of heat. The only way to find one suitable to your taste is to try them all. Produced from the central to northern regions of China.

Sichuan peppercorns (also known as Hua Jiao) These are actually the seed husks and not actual peppercorns. A deep pink colour when fresh, this colour deepens as the husks age, becoming dark red and eventually dark brown. The flavour also changes with age, highly perfumed and spicy when fresh, becoming musty and peppery when mature. Used in Sichuan peppercorn salt, and of course, many Sichuan dishes.

Star anise Shaped like a flower head, this spice is used in stews, braising, sauces. It is a major component of five-spice powder. Both the shell and seeds are used.

Cassia (Chinese cinnamon) Much less sweet smelling than its Middle Eastern and tropical cousin. This type of cinnamon is quite earthy but still recognisable as cinnamon. Used in stews, braising and five-spice powder.

Grass fruit (brown cardamom) An ovoid brown shell that contains many small seeds. Smells pungent and quite medicinal. Used to flavour stews and braises in conjunction with other spices. On its own it would render any dish unpalatable.

Fermented shrimp paste Made from grinding up fermented salted shrimps. This purplish-grey paste is used in sauces and stir-frying certain seafood dishes. Must be used sparingly as it is both salty and pungent (blachan can be used as a substitute).

Sesame paste Made from grinding up roasted white sesame seeds. Use in some cold dishes and as an accompaniment to some noodle dishes. Tahini cannot be used as a substitute as it is made from unroasted white sesame seeds.

Potato starch Extracted from potatoes, this is the main ingredient used for thickening sauces and coating food for deep frying. Potato starch maintains its consistency for a longer period than cornflour, giving better end results.

Water chestnut starch This is extracted from ground freshwater chestnuts. Used to thicken sauces/juices for fillings that are to be used in steamed dim sum. The sauce on cooling forms a jelly-like aspic and is easier to handle than one which has been thickened with potato starch.

Beancurd (tofu) Made from the 'milk' of soaked, ground soy beans. This 'milk' is simmered and then set with a small amount of gypsum. It is left to cool in large square containers and then cut into smaller 1kg squares and stored in water. Comes in different degrees of 'firmness', from silken tofu (used in soups and desserts), to 'firm' (used in most beancurd dishes) and 'pressed', where the beancurd has had nearly all its moisture removed through pressing to form a solid lump which can be treated like meat. Can also be marinated in this form to add flavour.

Deep-fried beancurd puffs Made from firm beancurd squares (3cm square), deep fried in oil until golden and all the moisture has evaporated. These balls of dry honeycombed beancurd are used in stews and braising for their ability to absorb flavour and liquid; they can also be cut open and stuffed with meat/fish or vegetables and steamed or deep fried.

Beancurd skin This is made from lifting the skin that forms during the simmering of soy bean 'milk'. The skins are then placed onto wooden dowels and allowed to dry. Very fragile, usually found in 18 inch (45cm) diameter circles. Can be used as a substitute for spring roll wrappers, or deep-fried and then reconstituted in water and used as a wrapper for meat/vegetables and steamed for dim sum.

Beancurd stick This is made from beancurd skin. Rather than allowing the skin to dry in a flat sheet, it is gathered up into a long roll and hung on wooden dowels to dry. Used in stews and braises, fried or unfried.

Fermented white beancurd This is made from cubes of salted beancurd that is preserved in distilled rice wine. It is very salty and pungent. Mainly used to add flavour to bland ingredients, such as poultry and pork, or to add additional flavour to plain green vegetables.

Fermented red beancurd This is actually made from squares of steamed taro that have been fermented with red rice, wine yeast and salt. Like fermented white beancurd, it is salty and pungent. Used as a component in Chinese roasting and braising sauces. Has a distinctive taste and aroma.

Preserved Sichuan vegetable This is in fact kohlrabi which has been preserved by using salt and chilli powder. It is dark green, mildly hot and very salty. It is usually thinly sliced and then briefly soaked in water to remove excess salt before use. Main use is shredded in various Sichuan stir fries, and as a flavouring in steamed meat dishes.

Pickled mustard Made from whole heads of mustard greens in brine which is then allowed to ferment to produce this salty sour vegetable. Usually thinly shredded and soaked in water to remove excess salt before use. Mainly used in stir-fried dishes that involve red meat or game. Also can be dry fried and finished off with sugar, sesame oil and white pepper and served as an appetiser.

Pickled shallots These small white bulbs are pickled in sweet white vinegar with red chillies. Quite pungent, they can be served on their own as an appetiser or shredded and used in cold salad-type dishes.

Sliced pickled ginger This is made from thinly sliced young root ginger, lightly salted and then pickled in a sweet rice vinegar. Chinese pickled ginger is pale yellow in colour, not pink as is Japanese pickled ginger.

Pickled plums These small yellow plums are pickled in brine and eventually turn brown and soft. The flesh is stripped off the stone and the pulp is used to flavour many dishes, most notably steamed spare ribs, and in the production of plum sauce.

Vegetables

3

Vegetables play a major part in the Chinese diet. The majority of Chinese people have always been farmers and are fortunate to live in a part of the world which is extremely fertile. The regions of China where people live and farm range from freshwater rivers and lakes to the coasts of seas and oceans, from deserts to tropical rainforests and bleak mountaintops to lush valleys. Any edible crop which can be grown is grown, and the surplus is sold to generate income to buy items which are not native to the region.

Most Chinese/oriental vegetables are easily obtainable from Chinese grocers these days and the choice available is staggering. Some items are still particular to specific regions of China and are very rarely seen, only available when in season, and if an importer is lucky enough to obtain stocks to export before they are invariably snatched up by the locals.

The following is a list of the oriental vegetables that are easily found in the UK, along with some interesting seasonal ones.

Angled luffa (See gwar) 絲瓜 Si gua (*Luffa cylindrical*) This is a melon (10–18 inches (25–45cm) long) that has thick skin and prominent ridges along its length. When young it has a pleasant green colour which darkens with age. It needs careful peeling before use, the ridges removed and some skin left on. Totally peeled and the melon will collapse into mush when cooked. It has a delicate sweet flavour and a spongy texture that goes well with seafood. It is usually stir fried with seafood or plainly steamed and dressed with soy sauce and ginger.

Aubergine (eggplant) 茄子 Qiezi (*Solanum melongena* v. *esculentum*) This type of vegetable comes in many different hues and shapes. The most common type in Europe is ovoid and a deep shiny purple. In Asia, the most common form is long and thin and deep lavender in colour. It is usually cooked using the steaming or braising method. It is deep-fried in very hot oil to colour it a light golden brown before the braising process.

Bamboo shoots 竹笋 Zhu sun (*Bambusa*) These are the tender young stems of a new season's growth of bamboo. They are now available fresh, whereas for many years they were only available canned, dried or preserved.

Fresh bamboo shoots contain a toxin that must be destroyed by boiling before they can be used in any recipes. Canned bamboo shoots are a much safer alternative, as they have been already processed and the toxin destroyed. However, a side effect of the canning process gives the bamboo a metallic taste that will taint an entire dish if it is not removed. Luckily, this is a very simple process; the bamboo shoots should be first boiled in clean water for 2–3 minutes (the water will turn a lemon yellow) and then refreshed before use. This will remove any trace of the metal taint.

Bean sprouts 緑豆芽 Lu douya The sprouts of the mung bean (*Phaseolus aureus*). Probably the vegetable most commonly associated with Chinese food. These white sprouts ($1\frac{1}{2}$ – 2 inches (3.5–5cm)) are best cooked by stir-frying; all other methods do not work well with this temperamental little sprout. They have a crunchy texture and slightly milky sweet taste.

Bitter melon (Foo gwar) 苦瓜 Ku gua (*Momordica charantia*) This summer vegetable is an acquired taste. It looks like a lumpy cucumber (5–10 inches (12–25cm) long) and is a pale green colour. It is extremely bitter in taste and is prized for its 'cooling' effect on the body. It is mainly used in soups and braised dishes. When ripe the bitterness increases, and the only way to tell whether or not it is ripe is by the colour of its seeds. Under-ripe ones have pale green or yellow seeds, while ripe ones have orange or red seeds.

Celery/Chinese celery 芹菜 Qin cai (*Apium graveolens* v. *dulce*) This is the Asian variety of celery. It is much thinner and more redolent of celery than its European counterpart, looking like long fennel tops. Quite fibrous in nature, it needs to be de-stringed before use. Mainly used in stir-fried dishes that contain red meat (beef, lamb, venison and duck), as the strong flavours of both complement each other. Also said to balance out the 'heat' of red meat.

Chayote (Chow chow, Buddha's palm melon) 合掌瓜 This is originally a South American vegetable. It is a flattened pear shape (4 inches (10cm) high), pale green colour with waxy skin and crispy, white firm flesh. Only slightly sweet, used in soups and can be stir fried on it own.

Chillies 辣椒 La jiao (*Capsicum annuum* v. *frutescens*) These fiery members of the capsicum (pepper) family are very useful for adding a kick to some Chinese dishes (central, northern and western). Care must be taken when using these, as it is very easy to forget and touch a sensitive part of your face after handling them and suffer chilli burn for several hours afterwards! The best way to overcome this is to wash your hands with detergent and *cold* water, not hot, as this will prevent your skin pores opening and allowing the chilli oils in. The two main types used in Chinese cooking are the red and green chillies. They generally occur in two sizes, 3–4 inches (8–10cm) or 1 inch (2.5cm). The smaller ones are called bird's eye chillies (Thai expression), although the literal Chinese translation for them is 'pointing to the sky peppers', a reference

to the way they point skyward on the bush. Green chillies are unripe red chillies, thus hotter than red chillies, as when they ripen less of the 'hot' chemicals are present. Finally, small chillies are hotter than large chillies.

Chinese black mushrooms (Dong Gu, Shiitake) 冬菇, 香菇 (*Lentinus edodes* v. *Shiitake*) These mushrooms are very common in Chinese cookery. They are now becoming available fresh, where previously they were only available dried or canned. There are two types available. One has an all-black cap and is relatively thin. The other has a much thicker cap that is 'crackled' in appearance. This type is known as 'flower' mushroom, as its appearance is like a chrysanthemum blossom. This is the more highly prized of the two types. They both have a strong meaty flavour. When buying dried mushrooms, check the date and the bottom of the packet as they are susceptible to attack from weevils, which can be seen if the packet is shaken so that they accumulate in the corners. When buying fresh ones, they should be firm and dry with a strong mushroom smell. If they are soft, wet and smell 'fruity', they are beginning to break down and should be avoided. Can be used in nearly all stir fried, steamed, braised, stewed and soup dishes.

A selection of vegetables (1)

Chinese box thorn (Gow gey choi) 枸杞 Gou qi (*Lycium chinense*) This green leaf vegetable comes on a tough woody stem (12–18 inches (30–45cm)) to which small dark green leaves are attached. The small leaves are removed and made into soup. It has a very mild tea-like flavour and the leaves become velvety on cooking.

Chinese broccoli/kale (Gai lan) 芥蘭 (*Brassica alboglabra*) This is probably the single most popular green leaf vegetable in Chinese cookery. It has a very similar appearance to Choi Sum (3–4 inches (7–10cm) high), except that it tends to be a darker spinach green. Also

its leaves tend to be fleshier and its flowerbuds contain a white flower. This will be the only way to tell them apart if you have both types (Choi Sum and Gai Lan) of a similar quality to hand. Unlike Choi Sum, Gai Lan is still an unknown green vegetable to most of the native UK populace, but once tasted, the crunchy green stem and meaty leaves are sure to be a hit. Only available from China by airfreight, but this is now a regular occurrence. The best ways to cook Gai Lan are blanching and stir-frying.

Chinese garlic chives (Gow choi) 韭菜 Jiu cai (*Allium tuberosum*) These pungent, flat, green grass-like leaves are a popular ingredient in soups and omelettes. They need to be cut into small lengths or they can be tough to eat.

Chinese leaf (Peking cabbage or Napa cabbage) 大白菜 Da bai cai (*Brassica pekinensis*) This cabbage is barrel shaped and can be 6–10 inches (15–25cm) long. The leaf stalks are white and the leaves crinkled and yellow. Best examples should be heavy for their size and not dry looking. The most famous dish in which Chinese leaf is used is 'Lionheads'. This is a dish of pork meatballs garnished with braised Chinese leaf, the meatballs representing the lion's head and the braised Chinese leaf the mane. Very good stir-fried on its own with ginger and seasonings.

Chinese spinach (Yin choi) 莧菜 Xian cai (*Spinacia oleracea*) This plant is usually sold whole. There are two varieties, one that is totally green, and one that has red centres on the oval leaves. The red centred variety is the more popular of the two. Young (smaller) specimens are preferred, as the larger ones can be a bit tough. Usually made into a tonic soup.

Choi sum 油菜心 You caixin (*Brassica parachinensis*) This is one of the two most popular green leaf vegetables in Chinese cookery. It has a bright apple green stem with tiny flower buds which contain a butter yellow flower. The colour of the flower is one way to distinguish it from Gai Lan. It is only just becoming available in some speciality vegetable sections of supermarkets. It has a fresh clean flavour that is best highlighted by simple blanching and dressing with oyster sauce. Can also be stir fried.

Chrysanthemum greens (Tong ho) 茼蒿 Tong hao (*Chrysanthenum spatisum*) These small (4–5 inch (10–12cm)) plants are an edible version of the popular house and garden plant. They have a deep green colour and slightly 'hairy' leaves. They have a distinctive chrysanthemum taste and are an acquired taste. Blanched or made into soup.

Coriander (Cilantro) 香菜, 芫茜 Xiang cai/yuanxi (*Coriandrum sativum*) A very versatile herb. Its seeds are used in spice mixtures, the root is used as a vegetable for stir-frying and spice pastes, and the leaves as a garnish for almost any dish. The whole plant is often used, boiled in water, in Chinese food medicine as a cure for sore throats. Very similar in appearance to flat leaf parsley (a cousin), except that the leaves of coriander are more delicate and rounded. Also, its distinctive scent identifies it.

Flowering garlic chives (Suen sum) 韭菜心 Jiucai xi (*Allium tuberosum* v. *odorum*) These are the jade green shoots from garlic that has reached the flowerbud stage (8–10 inches (2–25cm)). The stems are the edible part. They are juicy with a mild flavour and go well cooked as a vegetable with meat or poultry and seafood.

Fuzzy melon (Jeet gwar) 節瓜 Jie gua (*Benincasa acutangala*) This melon is long like a cucumber (8–10 inches (20–25cm)), but without the pointed ends. It is a pale green colour with hairy skin, the hairs in fact are quite stiff and sharp, and can cause irritation to the skin like nettles. It is best to wear rubber gloves when preparing this melon. Has a sharp, sweet waxy texture when cooked and is particularly good in soups or braised dishes.

Garlic 蒜 Suan (*Allium sativum*) Another indispensable ingredient in the Chinese kitchen. This is a white bulb with anything up to 20 cloves, all individually wrapped in its own skin. Its main purpose is to season oil before stir frying, but is also used whole (deep fried) in braised and double steamed dishes.

Ginger 姜 Jiang (*Zingiber officinale*) This rhizome is used extensively in Chinese cookery. It has many culinary and medicinal uses. Its appearance is lumpy, with a light brown skin (which thickens with age) and yellow flesh (which deepens in colour as it ages.). A good test to see whether or not ginger is young is to scratch its skin with your nail. If it comes off very easily and is juicy, then the ginger is young. This will become more difficult the older the ginger is. Ginger is used to season the oil before stir frying and to neutralise undesirable odours in meat and fish. Young ginger stems can be sliced and pickled, as can the young ginger buds that periodically appear if you keep root ginger for a few weeks in a brown paper bag in the fridge.

Old ginger still has its uses; it is used in stocks to eliminate undesirable odours and in some braised dishes where a more fiery ginger flavour is required.

Golden needle mushrooms (Enoki/Inoki) 金針菇 Jinzhen gu Mainly associated with Japanese cookery. They have very long stems topped off with a tiny cap, all a uniform straw yellow colour. They have a pleasant fruity smell (like pears) and a slightly chewy mild flavour. Only need brief cooking, otherwise they will collapse and toughen up. Used in stir fries and soups.

Golden needles (Gum jum) 金針, 黃花 Jinzhen, Huang hua (*Lilium tigrinum* v. *lancifolium*) These are the dried flowerbuds of a lily (3 inches/7cm). They have a musty, sharp odour and need to be soaked before use. Used in vegetarian dishes and the popular dish known as 'Mu-shu Pork'.

Jicama (Sah got) 沙葛 Sha ge (*Pueraria thomsoni*) Occasionally available in the UK. It looks like a giant beige-coloured head of garlic, about 6–7 inches (15–17cm) in diameter and 4–5 inches (10–12cm) high. It is actually a root vegetable; its taste is similar to that of water chestnut but less sweet. Mainly used for its texture in stir fries and in pickles.

Leeks (Dai suen) 韭葱 Jiu cong (*Allium porrum*) Mainly used in Northern Chinese cookery, where it is a staple vegetable. Usually cooked, stir fried with lamb.

Lettuce (romaine, iceberg) 生菜 Sheng cai (*Lactuca sativa*) Used to hold the fillings for lettuce wrap, simply blanched or stir-fried to maintain their crisp texture.

Lotus root 蓮藕 Lian ou (*Nelumbium nucifera* v. *speciosum*) This is the root of the water lotus plant. It is barrel shaped and pierced throughout internally with circular channels. If cut crosswise, it looks like a wheel or flower. It has a sweet taste with a firm/crunchy texture. Used in stir fries, stews, braised dishes and soups. Older roots become starchy, and from these, lotus root starch is extracted, which is used as a thickening agent.

Mange tout (Snow peas, Hor dow) 荷豆 He dou (*Pisum sativum*) These are young peapods that are still developing. They can be flat or cylindrical and fleshy. They need to be de-stringed before use in stir-fry dishes. Must be cooked briefly to maintain their crisp nature, or they will soften.

Mustard greens (Gai choi) 芥菜 Gai cai (*Brassica juncea*) Two types are available in the UK, one type is pale green, long and thin with thin crinkly leaves all along the length of the stem. This type is best for soups as there is very little substance to the leaves and they can be stringy. The second type is more round in shape like a cabbage, but has very thick meaty stems and pale green/yellow leaves. This type has a much better flavour, being slightly bitter, but cooling (this is an acquired taste). This type lends itself to many more cooking styles than the first type. It can be blanched and served with a little oyster or light soy sauce, braised with meat or cooked in a soup.

Peashoots (Dow mill) 豆苗 Dou miao These are the tender young shoots of mange tout or sugar snap peas (*Pisum sativum*), comprising two or three leaves with a tendril and flowerbud. Highly prized when available for their delicate flavour and perfume. Require only minimal cooking. Blanching and stir-frying are best.

Peppers (bell pepper) 椒 Jiao (*Capsium frutescen* v. *grossum*) A very versatile vegetable fruit, which lends itself to many cooking methods. Available in a range of bright colours. Usually used in stir-fried dishes to add colour and texture, can also be stuffed and braised.

Shallots 葱頭 Cong tou (*Allium ascalonicum*) Used in Chinese cookery as a small onion. Prized for its delicate taste and perfume. Mainly used in conjunction with fish/shellfish dishes and as a component in various sauces.

Silver ears (Wun yee) 銀耳 Yin'er (*Tremella fuciformis*) These are a type of edible fungus that grows on rotting wood. It is white in colour and full of holes, like a sponge. Usually only available dried or very rarely fresh, used mainly for its texture and 'cleansing' properties. When reconstituted from its dried state, it has a jelly-like appearance and texture. It is used in sweet and savoury soups and also in vegetarian dishes.

Snake beans (Dow gok) 長豆角 Chang dou jiao (*Vigna sesquipedalis*) Also known as yard-long beans, these are like elongated French beans (up to 24 inches (60cm)!). The uses for them are the same as for French beans when cut down to size. They are braised or finely chopped and incorporated into omelettes.

Soy bean sprouts 黃豆芽 Huang douya These are the sprouts of the soy bean (*Glycine hispidia*). They are longer ($3\frac{1}{2}$–$4\frac{1}{2}$ inches (8–11cm)) and thicker than the standard bean sprouts, and can be identified by the large yellow soy bean still attached to one end. These are tougher than mung bean sprouts and can take a lot more cooking. Definitely have a distinctive soy bean 'milk' taste. Usually dry-fried to remove some of their moisture before oil is added and the cooking process completed.

Spring onions (Scallions) 青葱 Qing cong (*Allium fistulosum*) These are essentially young underdeveloped onions. These long, green and white onions are very mild in taste and aroma. Used in many dishes as a vegetable or as a garnish. Because of their mildness, they can be used in nearly any dish (except with green leaf vegetables).

Straw mushrooms 草菇 Cao gu (*Volvariella volvacea*) So named, as they are cultivated on straw. Most commonly available tinned (young ones) or dried (older ones). Fresh specimens are unobtainable in the UK. The small tinned variety has the pleasant aspect of being filled with the canning liquor, so that when you bite into them, you get a spray of mushroom-flavoured liquid on the palate. The larger ones are usually sliced in half before use in stir-fries. They have a slippery texture, unlike the firm meaty texture of fresh straw mushrooms. The dried type are mainly used in soup; they need to be washed thoroughly, as they tend to trap a lot of sand under the cap.

Taro (Asian yam) 芋頭 Yutou (*Colocasia esculenta*) This is the only tuber that is commonly used in Chinese cookery. It is circular, has a thick dark brown skin and is about 5–6 inches (12–15cm) in length. It is available in two varieties: a white-fleshed type and one that has purple veins running through it. The purple-veined type is the more desirable one. Mainly used in braised dishes or steamed, mashed and made into a savoury pudding with preserved meats. It is also the main ingredient used in the manufacture of fermented red beancurd, a highly flavoured ingredient used in many dishes in this book.

Water chestnuts 荸薺, 馬蹄 Biqi, Mati (*Eleocharis tuberrosa*) This is the bulb of a water sedge plant. It is now available fresh, but is still more commonly available tinned. Its appearance is like a dark brown squat onion. It needs to be peeled before use and its colour should be white. If it is yellow or soft, this is a sign of decay. They have a sweet crunchy texture and can withstand long cooking without losing their texture. Used in stir fries, braised and stewed dishes. Older water chestnuts become starchy, and from these, water chestnut starch is obtained for use as a thickener. This thickening agent is used in bun fillings as it is more 'jelly-like' and will not liquefy on standing, as a great many thickeners will.

A selection of vegetables (2)

Watercress 洋菜 Yang cai (*Nasturtium officinale*) This delicate water plant is very popular as a tonic soup during the summer months. It is also eaten as a vegetable, simply blanched and dressed with oyster sauce (again!).

Water spinach (Toong choi/Oong choi) 蕹菜, 通菜 Weng cai/Tong cai (*Ipomoea reptans*) This is a green vegetable with a jointed hollow stem and long pointed leaves. Not really a member of the spinach family. When cooked it has a crunchy stem and soft smooth leaves. Shrinks a great deal when cooked. Mainly stir-fried or blanched.

White cabbage (Bok choi) 小白菜 Xiao baicai (*Brassica chinensis*) There are two variations of this cabbage, both are around 3–4 inches (8–10cm) high, fat and fleshy. The first has a white stalk with dark green leaves, the second has uniformly coloured light green stalks and leaves. The best examples are from China and Taiwan. The bok choi grown in Europe tends to be highly elongated and close to 10 inches (25cm) tall, rendering them stringy and tough. The best way to cook the Chinese varieties is to blanch in boiling salted water to which vegetable oil has been added, and dress with a good quality oyster sauce, or stir-fry with garlic and seasonings. Older specimens can be braised or turned into a nourishing soup made with salted duck's gizzards, dried figs, tangerine peel and apricot/peach kernels.

White radish (Mooli, Daikon) 蘿卜 Luo bo (*Raphanus sativus* v. *longipinnatus*) This root vegetable looks like a huge white carrot. It is generally 10–14 inches (25–35cm) long and can sometimes be larger! It should be heavy and firm with no signs of drying out or soft patches (especially near the top). Used in pickles, soups, braised and stewed dishes, and like the Taro, it can also be made into a savoury pudding. Also available is a green version, only used in soups and braised dishes.

Winter melon (Dong gwar) 冬瓜 Dong gua (*Benincasa hispida*) This large dark green melon is similar in appearance to a water melon. It has a slightly hairy, light green skin and can weigh from 2–40lb (1–20kg), with a girth to match (up to 20 inches (50cm) for a large specimen.). Large winter melons are hollowed out and filled with a clear soup and various meats and seafood, and then steamed for 3–5 hours to produce the famed winter melon pond, a banquet dish. Usually they are peeled and cut up to make soup. Can also be used in stews and braised dishes.

Wood ear (Mook yee) 木耳 Mu'er (*Auricularia auricula*) This is another tree-growing fungus that is highly prized for its texture. Its name comes from the fact that it looks, and its structure is uncannily like that of, an ear! Only available in dried form in the UK, where there are two types available, an all-black type, and one that is black on top with a white underside. They all need to be reconstituted before use. Used in stir fries, soups and braised dishes.

Yellow Chinese chives (Gow choi wong) 韭菜皇 Jiucai wang (*Allium tuberosum*) These are the same as the Chinese garlic chives, except they have been grown in the dark. This lightless growth has imbued these chives with an extremely pungent odour and tender leaves. Used the same way as the green garlic chives. Care needs to be taken when selecting these; make sure to check for signs of mushiness and sour odours.

Marinating Meat, Poultry, Fish and Seafood

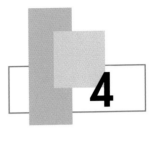

4

The Chinese marinate nearly all their meat, poultry, fish and seafood before cooking. There are some exceptions to this rule: fresh whole fish and seafood, that are live before being cooked, do not require marinating as they are thought to be perfect as they are, and it would be considered a sacrilege to hide their fresh sweetness with other flavours.

Fish is not always marinated before cooking; marinating is generally only used for large or tropical reef fish, which have a rough firm texture. The fish is usually filleted and either cut into slices or goujons before being marinated. Salt, sugar, potato starch, ginger, ground white pepper and wine are used. The potato starch is to give the fish a velvety smooth coating and 'mouth feel', and the ginger, white pepper and wine to counter any rank or strong fish odours.

Large shellfish, such as crabs, lobsters and molluscs need no marinating, as their delicate texture and flavour would be smothered.

Prawns, on the other hand, need to be marinated. They are most commonly available in frozen blocks (economical), and when defrosted they tend to be quite watery and flaccid. To cook these prawns as they are would result in a tough, dry texture, which would not be all that palatable. Fresh prawns are available, but the cost is prohibitive for many. The standard Chinese technique is to draw out any excess moisture from the prawns and firm them up by leaving them in a mixture of sugar, potato starch and bicarbonate of soda overnight. The prawns are then rinsed clean of this mixture, dried and marinated lightly with salt, sugar, ground white pepper and potato starch. This process, although long and quite tedious, results in prawns that are firm and 'crunchy' in texture. This may seem unnecessary to some, but once you have tasted a prawn marinated in this manner, your palate will find unmarinated prawns rather dry and flavourless.

Meat of any sort (except for that used in stews and braises and poultry that is to be cooked and served whole) is always marinated before cooking. Again, this is a cultural peculiarity of the Chinese in that any meat or poultry to be steamed or stir-fried should have a velvety texture on the palate. Meat or poultry that is simply cut up and cooked is considered to be 'rough' and 'sticks in the throat'.

The Chinese find the taste of unmarinated meat to be rank. There are two Chinese characters to describe this. The first is to describe the overwhelming taste of fresh blood (腥 xing), and the second is to describe the taste and smell of raw or cooked fat, especially that of lamb (臊 sao). The Chinese will go to great lengths to neutralise these smells, so that the true sweet taste of the meat comes through.

The general marinades for each type of meat, poultry, fish and shellfish can be found in Chapter 8.

In stir-frying, very lean meat is used, so that there is none of the sao smell or taste coming through. This means that a simple marinade is used to accentuate the taste of the meat and to make it tender and velvety.

In stews or braises where fat and connective tissues are required to give the finished dish the required texture and taste, the meat is subjected to various marinades and treatments to neutralise the fatty odours before cooking. This can be anything from blanching in boiling water, steeping in wine, pepper and ginger, to lightly scorching in a dry hot wok.

In deep-fried meat and poultry dishes, both the xing and sao aspects are not that important, as not so much the actual deep-frying but the accompanying sauces counter both of them. The sauces tend to be quite acidic and pungent, and mask these two unpleasant aspects, resulting in a flavoursome and appetising dish.

In steamed dishes, the xing and sao aspects are countered by the other ingredients that are used in the dish. These tend to be preserved, salted or pickled vegetables that have a strong distinctive flavour of their own, which complements and hides the two unwanted tastes. Nearly all steamed dishes use ginger as a counter to any unwanted flavours.

POTATO STARCH IN MARINADES

Potato starch is used in the marinades of various dishes in order to give the meat, poultry, fish or seafood a velvety texture. Potato starch is the first ingredient to be added and mixed in, followed by the other dry seasonings, and last of all, the oil. The potato starch is added in first and worked into the meat or poultry; in the case of fish and seafood, a thorough gentle mixing is all that is required to prevent the break-up of the delicate flesh.

This has the benefits of preventing the juices escaping when cooking, as they will be thickened by, and held by, the potato starch. This coating of thickened juices is what gives the meat, poultry, fish or seafood, its velvety texture on the palate.

The amount of potato starch used in the recipes should not be exceeded, as this will result in a glutinous mass (or mess!).

BICARBONATE OF SODA IN MARINADES

In many of the marinades used in this book, bicarbonate of soda is used. This is better known as an ingredient used in baking and patisserie. In the Chinese kitchen, it is invaluable as a tenderising agent. When used in a marinade, it will both help to break down the muscle fibres and cause the fibres to absorb more water, thus making them softer and more tender. It also prevents the water absorbed from leaching back out during the cooking process, so that the meat remains tender.

The other property of bicarbonate of soda is that it is hygroscopic, that is, it absorbs water, and was once used as a drying agent. This is the property at work when it is applied in the marinade of frozen prawns. The bicarbonate of soda draws out the excess water from the prawns, which are then taken up by the potato starch and sugar, firming up the prawns (see page 37, stage 1 in the marinating of frozen prawns).

Again, the quantities of bicarbonate of soda stated in the recipes must not be exceeded, as this will result in meat and poultry becoming flabby and waterlogged, and prawns losing their flavour and becoming overly crunchy, all texture and no taste.

Fish is never subjected to bicarbonate of soda, as this will cause it to toughen.

Creating
an Authentic
Chinese Dish

5

POINTS TO LOOK FOR IN CHINESE DISHES

Appearance

In stir-fried dishes, the food on the plate should look bright, fresh and clean, glossy, but not oily. There should be just enough sauce of the required consistency to cover all the ingredients, without leaving them swimming in it. There should not be any visible signs of oil on the plate from the sauce splitting. If this occurs it means either too much oil was used in the cooking process, or that the dish is dry and has been cooked too long. The garnish, if used, should be discreet and complement the dish; it should not occupy more than one-fifth of the plate.

The food in the finished dish should all be cut into the same shape and size in order to facilitate eating, that is, shredded meat and shredded vegetables together, diced meat and diced vegetables together, etc. A combination of two different forms would hinder the easy serving of food; for example, a dish consisting of cubed meat and cubed vegetables is easily served using a spoon, but if either one of the ingredients were shredded, then a spoon would only be able to pick up one or the other as would a pair of chopsticks (do you go for the cubes or the shreds?).

In steamed dishes, the food should look moist and juicy, the main ingredients should be lightly bound together, and the resulting steaming juices clear and fragrant. It should be literally 'steaming' as it is brought to the table to show its freshness, especially in the case of steamed whole fish.

Deep-fried dishes should look golden, dry and crisp if not finished in a sauce. If a dish has a greasy appearance, then the oil used to cook the items was not hot enough. Deep-fried dishes finished in a sauce should have just enough sauce to coat all the ingredients and should not be sitting in a pool of the said sauce.

Aroma

The finished dish should smell fragrant and mouth-watering. There should not be any burnt smells if the dish was stir fried, as this means that the wok was too hot, or not enough control over the heat was used, resulting in charring of the ingredients.

Steamed dishes should smell fresh and 'hot', indicating that they were just cooked to order.

Deep-fried dishes should smell 'freshly fried', indicating that they have been just cooked. If there is any hint of the smell of 'old oil', i.e. oil that has been used for too long without being changed or for cooking many different ingredients, that immediately renders the standard of the dish questionable, even if the ingredients are of the best possible quality.

Taste and texture

The taste of a dish is possibly the most important aspect. A dish can look a mess but if it smells and tastes fabulous, then all can be forgiven. A stir-fried dish should have a freshly cooked taste.

The main ingredient (meat, poultry, fish or seafood) should be just cooked, still juicy and have a velvety texture on the palate. The accompanying vegetables should be cooked but still retain a crisp bite. The whole dish should be of complementary flavours, with no one taste dominating the rest.

In steamed dishes, the main ingredient should be cooked, moist, soft and velvety. The accompanying preserved vegetables should still retain their texture and taste. The steaming juices should be a harmonious blend of the meat and vegetables.

Deep-fried dishes which have not been finished with a sauce should be crisp on the outside and juicy on the inside. The flavour of the deep-fried coating should complement the rich flavour of the main ingredient. The accompanying sauce should be sharp enough to cut through the richness of the dish and to complement the main ingredient instead of overwhelming it.

Braised and stewed dishes should have a rich flavour and the meat should be tender and melt in the mouth. As with its European counterparts, Chinese braised and stewed dishes use the tougher cuts of meat that are high in connective tissues to give the finished dish the require texture. The Chinese, more so than their European cousins, prize the gelatinous texture of slowly cooked meat. This can be seen in many of the braised dishes in the Chinese culinary repertoire.

The pursuit of texture – a Chinese eccentricity?

Texture plays a very important part in Chinese cuisine. This can be seen in the marinating of meat, poultry, fish and seafood before cooking to give the finished dish a 'better' texture. The use of various ingredients that have little taste, but high textural qualities (bamboo shoots, wood ear, water chestnuts) within the same dish to give different contrasts in texture, is also widely used and highly popular. Who wants to eat a dish that consists only of one texture?

Because the Chinese are largely Taoist or Buddhist, vegetarianism plays a large part of their lives. On holy days no meat is eaten, only vegetables, and as in the West, meat substitutes are available. These are made from wheat gluten into the form of chicken, beef or pork pieces, and highly seasoned and flavoured with fermented bean sauces to hide their true taste.

The Chinese separate texture into several different categories, these are:

- Soft (柔 rou) – referring to anything that is braised or stewed to tenderness, such as sea cucumber, dried scallops and abalone, or naturally soft, such as tofu.

- Velvety or slippery (not slimy) (滑 hua) – this term is applied to marinated stir-fried meat, poultry or fish. It is also used to describe certain braised ingredients that end up softly gelatinous but not sticky, such as fish lips, fish stomach and hair moss.

- 'Crunchy' (酥 su) – this term is used to define the texture/tenderness or 'bite' of marinated prawns and other ingredients of a firm nature.

Stocks and Soups  6

White Stock

Method

1. Chop up the chicken carcasses, rinse and place into stockpot. Cover with clean cold water and place onto stove.

2. Bring to a boil and then turn down to a low simmer, skimming all the time to remove the scum.

Measurements	Ingredients
5½ lb	Chicken carcasses
20 litre	Stockpot
	Water

3. When the scum begins to change to white, add 1 pint cold water. This will help to bring any remaining impurities to the surface. Continue skimming.

4. Simmer the stock for 3–5 hours, the stockpot should be three-quarters to two-thirds full.

5. The stock should be clear and golden. Carefully ladle off the clear top layer into a clean container. When the stock begins to go cloudy, it can be passed through muslin into a separate clean container.

Chef's Notes

- The reason for separating the stock in this way is two-fold: the clear top layer is generally used for clear broths and steamed soups, where clarity is important. The cloudy bottom layer can be used in cooking and soups where clarity is not important.

- Unsmoked ham and pork bones can also be used in white stock, but all fat needs to be removed before adding to the stockpot to avoid clouding up the stock. If jellied stock is required, blanched, scraped pork skin can be added and simmered with the other ingredients.

Brown Stock

Method

1. Rub the chicken carcasses with oil and roast at 190–200°C for 30–45 minutes, turning half way to ensure even colour.

2. Place all the ingredients into the stockpot and cover with cold water. Bring to the boil and follow the procedure for white stock.

Measurements	Ingredients
$5\frac{1}{2}$ lb	Roasted chicken carcasses
17 pint	Stockpot
2	Onions
24	White peppercorns
	Water

Chef's Notes

- The peppercorns and onions are used to counter the strong odour of roasted chicken fat. Roasted pork bones can also be used to add extra depth to the stock.

Basic Sweet Corn Soup

4 covers

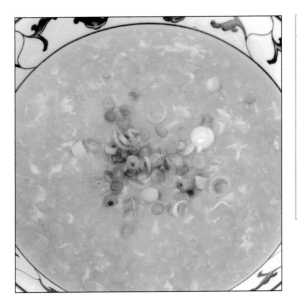

Measurements	Ingredients
20 floz	Good chicken stock
6 tbsp	Creamed corn
	Salt to taste
Pinch	Ground white pepper
	Slaked potato starch to thicken
1 small	Egg, beaten
	Sesame oil

Method

1. Put the stock and the creamed corn into a wok or saucepan and bring to a simmer.

2. Season the soup, taste and correct.

3. With constant stirring, add the slaked potato starch and a little water in a thin stream. Thicken the soup to the consistency of single cream.

4. Take the soup off the heat and carefully add the egg in a thin stream with slow stirring. The egg should form large flakes.

5. Add a few drops of sesame oil on top.

Chef's Notes

- Do not vigorously stir the soup when adding the egg as it will break up and the result will look like vomit. When thickening the soup, stop at the point when the corn is suspended in the soup. Too much thickener will result in a soup that resembles wallpaper paste, too little, and it will be watery. Adding the egg will also thicken the soup to a certain degree, so caution must be taken when thickening these soups.

Variations

- **Chicken and Sweet Corn Soup**: Add 2oz cooked diced chicken to the above recipe.
- **Crab and Sweet Corn Soup**: Add 2oz cooked white crabmeat to the above recipe.

Hot and Sour Soup

4 covers

Measurements	Ingredients
20 fl oz	Brown stock
Medium of each	Red and green chillies deseeded and sliced into rounds
1 tbsp	Light soy sauce
4 tbsp	Rice vinegar
	Dark soy, to colour
6 oz	Shredded ingredients (combination of carrot, fish cake, bamboo shoots, wood ear, straw mushroom, shiitake mushroom, Sichuan vegetable, ham, char siu, roast duck)
	Salt to taste
	Slaked potato starch
½ tsp	Ground white pepper
1 small	Egg, beaten
	Sesame oil

Method

1. Place the stock, chillies and light soy sauce into a wok or pan, bring to a low simmer and then add the vinegar. The stock will go cloudy at this point as the vinegar causes the fat to dissolve into the stock.

2. Correct the colour with dark soy sauce and then add the shredded ingredients. Bring back to a low simmer, taste and correct the seasoning with salt and vinegar.

3. Thicken with slaked potato starch to thin cream consistency. Add the ground white pepper, remove from the heat and slowly add the beaten egg in a thin stream, stirring into the soup to form egg flowers.

4. Add a dash of sesame oil.

Chef's Notes

- Traditionally, this dish was thickened with duck's blood, and the heat was from white pepper rather than chillies.

- This soup is served with Chinese red vinegar and chilli oil, so that the diner can adjust the level of acidity and heat to suit their taste.

Variations

- The shredded ingredients can be substituted with seafood to produce a more high class soup. In this case, the level of acidity and chilli heat needs to be moderated to prevent the flavours of the seafood from being overwhelmed.

Winter Melon and Shiitake Mushroom Soup

4 covers

Method

1. Place the chicken stock, diced winter melon and ginger into a wok or stainless steel pan. Bring to a low simmer and skim off any impurities.

2. Simmer for 5 minutes until the melon is just beginning to soften, then add the diced shiitake mushrooms. Bring back up to a simmer and cook for a further minute.

3. Remove the ginger and season to taste with the salt and white pepper. The mushrooms will have coloured the soup a light coffee tone.

4. Add a dash of sesame oil to the bottom of the serving bowl and carefully ladle over the soup.

Measurements	Ingredients
20 fl oz	Chicken stock
6 oz	Winter melon (peeled and diced)
2 thin slices	Ginger
2 oz	Shiitake mushrooms (diced)
	Salt and ground white pepper to taste
	Sesame oil

Chef's Notes

- The winter melon should still be a bright green when cooked. This means that the dice need to be around $\frac{1}{4}$ inch (6mm) square in order to be cooked in the stated cooking time above. If cooked too long, the winter melon will become translucent, absorb the colour of the soup and become brown.

Winter Melon Purée Soup

4 covers

Method

1. In a wok or stainless steel pan, add 1 tbsp oil and gently fry the ginger until lightly golden.

2. Add the diced winter melon and cook for 1 minute. Add the chicken stock and bring to a

Measurements	Ingredients
1 tbsp	Oil
2 thin slices	Ginger

continued over →

fast simmer, skimming to remove any impurities and oil.

...continued

3. Simmer until the winter melon is just cooked (the point of a knife easily pierces the winter melon). Remove the ginger slices and then purée the mixture using a hand blender.

4. Pass through a chinois (a fine mesh conical sieve) into a clean pan, taste and correct seasoning. If too watery, thicken with potato starch.

5. Add a few drops of sesame oil just before serving.

6 oz	Winter melon, peeled and diced into $\frac{1}{4}$ inch dice
20 fl oz	Chicken stock
	Salt and ground white pepper to taste
	Slaked potato starch
	Sesame oil

Chef's Notes

• Do not overcook the melon or cover the pan, otherwise the soup will lose its colour.

Variations

• After passing the soup, 2oz marinated chicken purée can be stirred into the soup and cooked through on a gentle heat.

• Chayote or Chow Chow, or marrow can be substituted for winter melon.

Chicken and Mushroom Broth

4 covers

Method

1. Place the chicken stock into a wok or stainless steel pan. Bring slowly to a simmer and season with salt.

2. Add the prepared mushrooms and the cooked chicken breast. Bring back up to a slow simmer and cook for 1 minute. Remove from the heat.

3. To four soup bowls, add a dash of dark soy sauce, sesame oil, ground white pepper and chopped spring onions.

4. Carefully ladle over the soup and divide the chicken and the mushrooms evenly between the bowls.

Measurements	Ingredients
20 fl oz	Clear chicken stock
2 oz	Assorted mushrooms (enoki, shimeiji, shiitake, oyster)
4 oz	Marinated chicken breast strips, cooked by poaching in seasoned chicken stock
	Salt to taste
	Dark soy sauce (to finish)
	Ground white pepper (to finish)
	Sesame oil, to finish
1	Spring onion (chopped)

Chef's Notes

- Do not allow this soup to boil as it will go cloudy and spoil the end result.

Variations

- **Chicken and Noodle Soup**: Remove the mushrooms and dark soy sauce. Substitute 2oz cooked Yi noodles. Follow as before.

Won Ton Soup

4 covers

Method

1. Place $3\frac{1}{2}$ pints water into a pan and bring to a very gentle simmer. Add a tablespoon of salt and poach the won tons for 4–5 minutes. Drain and keep warm.

2. Place the chicken stock into a clean pan and bring to a low simmer. Season with salt. Keep hot.

3. Divide the spring onions into four soup bowls, to each add a dash of sesame oil and ground white pepper. A dash of dark soy sauce can be added if required.

Measurements	Ingredients
20 fl oz	Chicken stock
12	Won tons (see following recipe)
2	Spring onions, washed and chopped
	Salt to taste
	Sesame oil, ground white pepper and dark soy sauce (optional to finish)

4. Place three cooked won tons into each bowl, and ladle over the hot stock. Gently stir and serve immediately.

Variations

- The fillings for the won tons can be varied to suit your own tastes.

Won Tons

Method

1. Combine the pork, prawns and mushrooms in a clean bowl, add the marinade ingredients and mix well. Cover and place in the fridge for a minimum of 4 hours, and a maximum of 24 hours.

2. Remove from the fridge and add the egg yolk. Mix well.

3. Cut the corners off the won ton wrappers to form octagons. Place a teaspoon of filling into the middle of each wrapper, draw up the edges to enclose the filling and carefully press firmly above the filling to seal. The won ton should look like a small drawstring purse.

4. Deep-fry at 180° C for 3–4 minutes until golden and crispy, and serve with sweet and sour sauce, or gently simmer in boiling water for 4–5 minutes for use in won ton soup. They have to be pre-cooked as the colouring in the wrappers will cloud the broth.

Measurements	Ingredients
250g	Fatty pork loin chops (roughly chopped)
150g	Raw tiger prawns (shelled, de-veined, roughly chopped)
6 small	Shiitake mushrooms (diced, blanched and drained)
40–50	Won ton wrappers
1	Egg yolk
Marinade	Ingredients
1 tsp	Salt
2 tsp	Sugar
$\frac{1}{4}$ tsp	Pepper
2 tsp	Potato starch
$\frac{1}{4}$ tsp	Bicarbonate of soda
1 tsp	Shao xing wine
1 tsp	Sesame oil

Basic Preparations  **7**

Cashew Nuts

For use in Chicken with Cashew Nuts

Method

1. Bring a wok half full of water to the boil. Add salt and sugar to the water so that it tastes salty and slightly sweet. Add 1 tsp five-spice powder and the cashew nuts. Boil for 10 minutes. Drain and place on kitchen paper to absorb the excess moisture.

2. Bring an empty wok to a high heat and add oil so that it is one-third full. Heat the oil to around 140–150°C, and carefully add the nuts. The oil should not sizzle but bubble gently.

Measurements	Ingredients
	Water
	Salt
	Sugar
1 tsp	Five-spice powder
4 oz	Raw cashew nuts
	Vegetable oil for deep-frying

3. The purpose is to force out the remaining water. The oil will look cloudy at this point as it will be saturated with water in the form of steam. Stir the nuts constantly. Do not allow them to rest on the bottom as they will burn.

4. If the oil is not moving at all, increase the heat until it begins to bubble, then turn down the heat to maintain the constant gentle bubbling.

5. When the oil clears, this means that all the water has been expelled from within the nuts, and they will rapidly begin to brown. Watch the nuts carefully at this stage. When they have reached a pale golden colour, remove them and drain on some kitchen paper. They will continue to brown, which is why you have to remove them at the pale brown stage.

6. Cool and store in an airtight container.

Spiced Salt (1)

Method

1. In a wok, slowly heat the salt with continual stirring until it changes colour and you can smell a metallic tang.

Measurements	Ingredients
2 oz	Salt
$\frac{1}{4}$ tsp	Five-spice powder
$\frac{1}{8}$ tsp	Ground white pepper

2. Remove from the heat and add the five-spice powder and white pepper, stirring all the while. The salt should be evenly speckled with the brown of the five-spice powder. Remove any lumps.

3. Pour into a bowl and leave to cool.

Spiced Salt (2 – Pepper Salt)

Method

1. Follow the above procedure.

Measurements	Ingredients
2 oz	Salt
$\frac{1}{4}$ tsp	Finely ground white pepper
$\frac{1}{4}$ tsp	Finely ground black pepper

Spiced Salt (3 – The Classic One)

Method

1. Follow the above procedure.

Measurements	Ingredients
2 oz	Salt
$\frac{1}{4}$ tsp	Farchiew (Sichuan peppercorns) powder

Deep-fried Garlic Flakes

Method

1. Soak the dried garlic flakes in the hot water for 20 minutes, then drain on kitchen paper to absorb excess moisture.

2. Bring a wok one-third full of oil to 140–150°C and add the garlic flakes. The oil will become cloudy with the water vapour, so keep stirring the garlic flakes until the cloudiness disappears.

3. When the flakes are a golden brown remove and drain them on some kitchen paper.

4. Cool and store in an airtight container.

Measurements	Ingredients
2 oz	Dried garlic flakes
	Hot water
	Vegetable oil for deep-frying

Chef's Notes

• These flakes are a good substitute for fresh garlic in stir-fry recipes as their flavour is more intense and nutty.

• Save the oil for use in seafood dishes.

Chinese Mushrooms

Method

1. Break off the stems of the dry mushrooms. Place into a saucepan and half fill with water.

2. Bring to the boil, and continue to boil for 2 minutes. Drain and cool slightly. Squeeze out the excess liquid and discard – it is bitter.

3. In a wok slowly fry the garlic and ginger to release their aromas, then add the mushrooms, sugar, white pepper and Shao Xing wine. Cook slowly for 1 minute.

4. Add water to cover the mushrooms, bring to the boil and simmer for 1½–2 hours or until tender, adding more water if necessary.

5. If there is a lot of liquid left, i.e. two-thirds to three-quarters remaining, reduce by half.

Measurements	Ingredients
4 oz	Dried Chinese mushrooms (flower type preferred)
2 cloves	Garlic, crushed
3 slices	Ginger
1 oz	Yellow rock sugar
	White pepper
1 tbsp	Shao Xing wine
	Dark soy sauce
	Salt
Dash	Sesame oil
1 tbsp	Oil

Adjust the colour with dark soy sauce. Taste and correct the seasoning, adding soy sauce, white pepper and sesame oil if to be eaten as a vegetarian dish, otherwise leave to cool for use in other dishes.

Chef's Notes

• Salt is not added to the dry mushrooms during the cooking process as this will inevitably toughen up the mushrooms and not tenderise them as the rock sugar does.

Prawn Paste

Method

1. Place the tiger prawns in a bowl and add 2 tablespoons potato starch. Mix well and leave for 5 minutes.

2. Mince the pork back fat.

3. Rinse the prawns under cold water in a colander until all the potato starch is gone. Dry thoroughly with a clean tea towel or kitchen tissue.

4. Place the prawns onto a chopping board, and using the flat side of a cleaver, smash the prawns into a pulp and then chop them until they become a fine paste.

Measurements	Ingredients
16 oz	Black tiger prawns (shelled and de-veined)
3 tsp	Potato starch
4 oz	Pork back fat
$\frac{1}{2}$ tsp	Salt
$\frac{1}{4}$ tsp	Sugar
1	Egg white
A large pinch	White pepper

5. Scrape the paste into a bowl and add the pork fat and the rest of the ingredients. Stir with your hands in one direction only until it becomes sticky.

6. Gather up the paste in one hand, then fling it back into the bowl. Repeat 10 times. Place back into the bowl and cover. Place into a fridge to chill and firm up. Use as required.

Curry Powder Paste

Method

1. Combine the oil and curry powder in a saucepan or wok.

2. Slowly heat up until it begins to fizz, stirring constantly.

3. Cook for 1 minute until fragrant. Remove from heat and add the fresh curry powder and stir in.

4. Cool immediately in cold water.

5. Pour into a glass jar and store in a fridge until required.

Measurements	Ingredients
2 oz	Curry powder (Madras or Malaysian)
4 fl oz	Oil
1 tbsp	Fresh curry powder

Chow Mein Sauce

15–20 portions

Method

1. Combine all the ingredients and refrigerate. Use as required.

Measurements	Ingredients
20 fl oz	Oyster sauce
26 fl oz	Shao Xing wine
6–8 tbsp	Sugar (according to taste)
6 tbsp	Dark soy sauce
1 tsp	White pepper
$1\frac{3}{4}$ pints	Stock

Sauces and Marinades

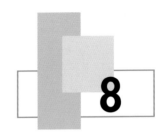

8

Black Bean Sauce (1)

For stir-frying

Method

1. Soak the black beans in warm water to remove the excess salt and grit. Drain and rinse again. Set aside.

2. Heat 1 tablespoon oil in a wok and gently fry the ginger for 1 minute. Add the garlic and continue for a further minute. Add the chilli and cook for 1 minute more. Add the black beans and stir-fry gently until fragrant, but not burnt.

3. Remove from the heat and place into a bowl. Add the remaining ingredients and mix well. Cover with cling film and steam for 30 minutes. Cool and store in the fridge until use.

Measurements	Ingredients
1 small bowl	Black beans (approx. 2oz)
1 tbsp	Ginger (finely chopped)
2 cloves	Garlic (finely chopped)
$\frac{1}{2}$	Red chilli (chopped)
1 tsp	Crushed fried garlic flakes
1 tbsp	Shao Xing wine
$1\frac{1}{2}$ tsp	Sugar
1 tsp	Light soy sauce
Pinch	Ground white pepper
Dash	Sesame oil

Black Bean Sauce (2)

For steaming

Method

1. Place all the ingredients except the potato starch into a bowl or mortar, and grind into a paste. Taste and correct the seasoning. Add the potato starch and mix thoroughly. Add an additional 2 teaspoons potato starch before use.

Chef's Notes

- If using this sauce to steam an oily fish, 2 teaspoons chopped fresh lemon can be added to counter the oiliness, as can 1 teaspoon chopped dried tangerine peel.

Measurements	Ingredients
2 tbsp	Fermented black beans
2 cloves	Garlic
1 tsp	Minced ginger
1 tsp	Red chilli (chopped) (optional)
1 tbsp	Light soy sauce
1 tsp	Shao Xing wine
$1\frac{1}{2}$ tsp	Sugar
Dash	Sesame oil
Pinch	White pepper
$\frac{1}{4}$ tsp	Potato starch

Braising Sauce

Method

1. Fry the shallots in oil until soft but not coloured.

2. Add all the pastes and sauces and cook thoroughly until hot.

3. Leave to cool in a container and refrigerate until ready to use.

Measurements	Ingredients
2	Shallots (minced)
10 oz	Crushed yellow bean sauce
3 oz	Sesame paste
3 oz	Hoisin sauce
2 squares	Red bean curd (mashed)
1 tbsp	Oil

Chicken Marinade (1)

For stir-frying 16 oz chicken

Measurements	Ingredients
1 tsp	Salt
$\frac{1}{2}$ tsp	Sugar
Pinch	Ground white pepper
1 tsp	Potato starch
Pinch	Bicarbonate of soda
2 tbsp	Water
1 tbsp	Oil
Dash	Sesame oil

Chicken Marinade (2)

For steaming 16 oz chicken

Measurements	Ingredients
1 tsp	Salt
$\frac{1}{2}$ tsp	Sugar
1 tsp	Soy sauce
1 clove	Garlic (sliced)
2 slices	Ginger (shredded)
2 tsp	Potato starch
Pinch	Ground white pepper
2 tsp	Shao Xing wine
$1\frac{1}{2}$ tbsp	Oil
Dash	Sesame oil

Beef Marinade (1)

For stir-frying 16 oz beef

Measurements	Ingredients
1 tsp	Salt
$\frac{1}{2}$ tsp	Sugar
2 tsp	Potato starch
$\frac{1}{8}$ tsp	Bicarbonate of soda
1 tsp	Soy sauce
Pinch	Ground white pepper
2 tsp	Rose liqueur
4 tbsp	Water
1 tbsp	Oil
Dash	Sesame oil

Beef Marinade (2)

For stir-frying 16 oz beef fillet

Measurements	Ingredients
1	Egg
2 tsp	Potato starch
2 tsp	Rose liqueur
$\frac{1}{2}$ tsp	Ginger juice
1 tsp	Dark soy sauce
1 tsp	Salt
$\frac{1}{2}$ tsp	Sugar
1 tbsp	Water
1 tbsp	Oil
Pinch	Ground white pepper
Dash	Sesame oil

Pork Marinade

For stir-frying 16 oz pork

Measurements	Ingredients
1 tsp	Salt
$\frac{1}{3}$ tsp	Sugar
2 tsp	Potato starch
$1\frac{1}{2}$ tbsp	Water
$\frac{1}{8}$ tsp	Bicarbonate of soda
Pinch	White pepper
1 tbsp	Oil
Dash	Sesame oil

Duck Marinade

For stir-frying 16 oz duck

Measurements	Ingredients
1 tsp	Salt
$\frac{1}{2}$ tsp	Sugar
1 tsp	Soy sauce
1 tsp	Rose liqueur
$1\frac{1}{2}$ tsp	Potato starch
$\frac{1}{8}$ tsp	Bicarbonate of soda
1 tbsp	Water
Pinch	Ground white pepper
1 tbsp	Oil
Dash	Sesame oil

Sweet and Sour Sauce (1)

Method

1. Combine all the ingredients in a wok, bring to the boil and simmer for 5–10 minutes. Thicken with potato starch and water.

Measurements	Ingredients
10 fl oz	White rice vinegar/distilled malt vinegar
1 tbsp	Worcester sauce
8 oz	Slice sugar
2 fl oz	Tomato ketchup
	Salt to taste
$\frac{1}{2}$	Lemon (juice only)
	Potato starch and water for thickening

Sweet and Sour Sauce (2)

Method

1. Combine all the ingredients in a wok, bring to the boil and simmer for 5–10 minutes. Thicken if necessary.

Chef's Notes

- Pineapple juice from the tinned fruit that is integral to sweet and sour dishes can also be added. If so, increase the cooking time by 10–15 minutes to reduce the excess liquid.

Measurements	Ingredients
10 fl oz	White rice vinegar/distilled malt vinegar
1 fl oz	Tomato ketchup
1 oz	Sour plums (mashed)
5 oz	Slice sugar
1 fl oz	Worcester sauce
$1\frac{1}{2}$ fl oz	Brown/fruity sauce
	Salt to taste

Chilli Oil

Method

1. To a clean wok, add the chopped chillies, garlic, shrimps and shallots. Add enough oil to cover the ingredients, and slowly turn up the heat. When the ingredients begin to sizzle, turn the heat down so that the ingredients are gently simmering.

2. With constant stirring, gently cook the ingredients until they are soft and melting. This should take about 10–15 minutes.

3. Remove the wok from the heat and add the shrimp paste. Stir vigorously to incorporate the paste into the oil and ingredients.

4. Allow to cool. Taste and correct the seasoning with sugar and soy sauce. You can tell when the chilli oil is ready as it becomes a deep red.

Measurements	Ingredients
9 oz, large	Red chillies (finely chopped, seeds included)
2–3	Bird's eye chillies (finely chopped, seeds included)
2 tbsp	Garlic (chopped)
1 oz	Dried shrimps (chopped)
4 oz	Shallots (chopped)
	Vegetable oil
1 tbsp	Fermented shrimp paste (solid or soft)
	Soy sauce
	Sugar to taste

Chinese Curry Sauce Base

Method

1. Pour the oil into the wok and add the garlic, onion, chilli and ginger. Cook on a low heat until the onion softens and begins to colour.

2. Add the curry powder and cook for about 1 minute until fragrant.

3. Add the chopped fruit and cook slowly for 5 minutes. Then add the water and bring to a boil. Turn down the heat, add the salt and simmer until the fruit is soft and mushy (about 10–15 minutes).

4. Turn up the heat and slowly reduce the liquid by a half. Stir occasionally to prevent sticking.

5. Purée using a hand blender and pass thorough a sieve to remove any fibres. Pour into a container and leave to cool.

Measurements	Ingredeints
7 fl oz	Oil
2 cloves	Garlic (minced)
1 small	Onion (chopped)
1	Red chilli (chopped)
1 tbsp	Ginger (chopped)
3 oz	Malaysian curry powder
16 oz	Ripe fruit (apples, bananas, etc., chopped)
30 fl oz	Water
2 tsp	Salt

Chef's Notes

- To use as curry sauce, it is necessary to thin out the base with coconut cream and coconut milk and correct the seasoning.

Peking Chilli Sauce

Method

1. Gently heat the oil in a wok and slowly cook the garlic and shallots until they are soft.

2. Add the chilli and cook slowly for 1 minute until the oil goes red. Add the rest of the ingredients and cook slowly for 2–3 minutes until gently bubbling.

3. Pour into a bowl, taste and correct the seasoning with soy sauce.

Measurements	Ingredients
2 tbsp	Oil
3 cloves	Garlic (minced)
2	Shallots (minced)
1	Red chilli (puréed)
4 tbsp	Hot bean sauce
1 tbsp	Tomato purée or tomato sauce
1 tbsp	Chilli oil
1 tbsp	Crushed yellow bean sauce
2 tbsp	Sugar
1 tbsp	Sesame oil
	Soy sauce to taste

Simple Spicy Sauce

Method

1. Add the oil to a wok and fry the garlic and the chilli until pungent. Add the five-spice powder and cook for 10 seconds (important – do not burn the five-spice powder).

2. Add the remaining ingredients and bring to a boil. Simmer until the sauce is reduced by a quarter and looks syrupy.

3. Turn off the heat and add the pepper and the sesame oil. Pour into a bowl and cool.

Chef's Notes

• Use in shredded spicy beef or as a dipping sauce for quail/ribs in spice salt.

Measurements	Ingredients
2 tbsp	Oil
2 cloves	Garlic (finely chopped)
$\frac{1}{2}$	Red chilli (chopped)
$\frac{1}{4}$ tsp	Five-spice powder
4 tbsp	Malt vinegar
3 tbsp	Sugar
2 tbsp	Tomato sauce
1 tbsp	Worcester sauce
2 tbsp	Lemon juice
Dash	Sesame oil and white pepper to finish

Roasting Sauce/Marinade

Method

1. Place all ingredients from A into a stainless steel bowl and mix together.

2. Place all ingredients from B into a wok, and slowly cook until fragrant. Add the mixed ingredients from A. Bring to the boil slowly and simmer for 1 minute.

3. Transfer to a clean stainless steel bowl and add 1 tablespoon sesame oil to seal the surface. Cool and use as directed in recipes.

Measurements	Ingredients A
20 fl oz	Hoisin sauce
6 oz	Yellow bean sauce
6 oz	Sesame paste
6 oz	Oyster sauce
4 squares	Fermented red bean curd and juice
10 oz	Sugar
10 fl oz	Soy sauce
1 tsp	Five-spice powder
Measurements	Ingredients B
4 whole	Dried tangerine skins (soaked, scraped and minced)
10 cloves	Garlic (finely chopped)
10	Shallots (peeled and finely chopped)
6 tbsp	Oil

Chilli, Ginger and Tomato Sauce

Method

1. Add the tomato base ingredients to a stainless steel pan.

2. Bring to the boil and then reduce the heat and simmer until all the liquid has evaporated, and all that is left is a thick pulp.

3. Leave to cool.

Tomato Base	Ingredients
2 oz	Shallots (chopped)
9 oz	Tomatoes (peeled, deseeded and chopped)
4 fl oz	Rice vinegar
2 oz	Sugar

continued over →

4. Sweat off the shallots and garlic in the oil.

5. Add the chillies and cook slowly for 15–20 minutes until soft.

6. Add the ginger and cook slowly until nearly all the liquid has gone.

7. Add the tomato base and cook until all liquid is virtually gone.

8. Pour into a large stainless steel bowl and season with the fish sauce, sugar and vinegar.

9. Cool and cover. Leave to mature for about a week before use.

...continued

Main sauce	Ingredients
4 oz	Shallots (chopped)
2 oz	Garlic (chopped)
10 fl oz	Oil
20 oz	Red chillies (deseeded and chopped)
7 oz	Root ginger (scraped and grated)
	Sugar, fish sauce and vinegar to season

Cold Dishes

Shanghai 'Smoked' Fish

Method

1. Place all the marinade ingredients in a wok and bring slowly to the boil. Cook slowly until the sugar has dissolved.

2. Pour the marinade into a large bowl and allow to cool.

3. Once the marinade has cooled, place the fish into it. If the marinade does not cover the fish, turn every 2–3 hours. Marinate for 24 hours, or overnight.

4. Remove the fish from the marinade, dry thoroughly with tissue and place on a wire rack to air dry until just touch dry.

5. Heat a wok of oil and deep-fry the fish for 3–4 minutes until golden. Remove and drain.

Measurements	Ingredients
2 lb	Firm white fish darnes
	Oil for deep-frying
6 oz	Chinkiang vinegar (to finish)
Marinade	Ingredients
1 pint	Light soy sauce
1 pint	Water
8 oz	Sugar
2 pieces	Dried tangerine peel
3	Spring onions (bruised)
1 large piece	Ginger (crushed)
Large pinch	White pepper

6. Place the marinade in a wok and bring slowly to the boil, skimming continuously. Slowly reduce the marinade to half its original volume, or until syrupy. Cool and add the vinegar.

7. Pour over the fried fish and allow to steep for 3–4 hours.

8. Remove the fish and drain. The remaining liquid can be reduced down further and used to glaze the fish.

Bang Bang Chicken

Method

1. Combine all the sauce ingredients in a bowl and set aside.

2. In a dry wok, gently dry-fry the sesame seeds until golden brown. Place into a bowl and set aside to cool.

3. Rub the chicken with the salt, wine and sesame oil, place onto a plate and steam for 25–30 minutes.

4. When the chicken has cooled, remove the skin and bones and shred the meat.

5. Place the shredded cucumber, coriander leaves and spring onion onto a plate, pile on the chicken, pour over the sauce and sprinkle with the sesame seeds. To serve, mix at the table in front of your guests.

Sauce	Ingredients
1 tbsp	Sesame paste
1 tbsp	Chilli oil
$\frac{3}{4}$ tsp	Sugar
2 cloves	Garlic (minced)
$\frac{1}{4}$ tsp	Roasted Sichuan pepper
3 tbsp	Light soy sauce
2 tbsp	Chinkiang vinegar and red rice vinegar
2 tbsp	Chicken stock (optional)
Measurements	**Ingredients**
1 tbsp	Sesame seeds
2 (approx. 12oz)	Chicken breasts
2 tsp	Salt
1 tbsp	Shao Xing wine
1 tsp	Sesame oil
8 oz	Cucumber (deseeded and shredded)
1 handful	Coriander leaves
2	Spring onion whites (shredded)

Hand Torn Chicken

Method

1. Bring a large pan of boiling water (with the ginger) to the boil. Add the chicken and poach, 20 minutes for the breast, or 45 minutes for the whole chicken. Remove and allow to cool down in the stock.

Measurements	Ingredients
1 inch	Ginger (bruised)
1 whole (approx. 2lb)	Chicken breast on the bone or

2. Remove the skin from the chicken and pull the meat away from the bones in large strips/pieces, keeping the dark and white meat separate.

3. In a wok, heat the salt on a low heat until it turns a silvery/grey colour. Remove the wok from the heat and allow to cool for 2–3 minutes. Add the oil, sesame oil and heat until smoking. Remove from the heat, cool slightly, then add the stock and ginger powder and gently reheat.

4. As the sauce comes to a simmer, add the dark meat, and stir the chicken around to absorb the flavours and until it is heated through. Add the white meat and turn gently to absorb the flavours and continue until all the chicken is piping hot.

5. Place the ho-fun and spring onion whites onto a plate; add the chicken, along with some of the sauce, over the onions. Garnish with the coriander leaves.

Measurements	Ingredients
1 whole (approx. $3\frac{1}{2}$ –4 lb)	Chicken
2 tsp	Salt
5 fl oz	Oil
4 fl oz	Sesame oil
4 fl oz	Chicken stock
1 tbsp	Sand ginger powder
8 oz	Ho-fun (steamed before use)
6	Spring onion whites (shredded)
3 bunches	Coriander (leaves only)

Chef's Notes

• Halve the above ingredients if just using chicken breast.

Drunken Chicken (1)

Method

1. Bring a pan of water to the boil. The water should be deep enough to cover the chicken. Place the chicken in the water and return to the boil, turn down the heat and poach for 25–30 minutes.

2. Remove the chicken from the water and drain. Leave to cool. Heat the chicken stock gently; add the crushed ginger, spring onion, sugar, salt and white pepper. The stock should taste slightly salty. Add more stock if too salty and leave to infuse for 10–15 minutes. Set aside to cool.

Measurements	Ingredients
Approx. $1\frac{1}{2}$ lb	Chicken
$\frac{1}{2}$ pint	Chicken stock (clear)
2 slices	Ginger (crushed)
1	Spring onion (crushed)
1 tsp	Sugar
2 tsp	Salt
$\frac{1}{8}$ tsp	Ground white pepper
3 tbsp	Rose liqueur
3 tbsp	Shao Xing wine
	Coriander leaves to garnish
	Sesame oil to garnish

3. Chop the chicken into bite-sized pieces and arrange on a plate. Place a bowl over the chicken then invert it into the bowl. Pour the warm stock over, using a sieve to remove the bits of crushed ginger and onion. Finally add the two wines and cool. Cover and place in the fridge overnight to marinate.

4. To serve, drain off the marinade, if not set, and turn out onto a plate. Garnish with coriander and a drizzle of sesame oil.

Drunken Chicken (2)

Method

1. Blanch the pork rind and add to the chicken stock, along with the crushed ginger and spring onion. Bring slowly to the boil and simmer gently for 30 minutes to extract the gelatine from the pork rind. Strain to remove the rind and bits of ginger and spring onion. Add the sugar, salt and pepper, taste, and correct the seasoning. The stock should taste slightly salty. Set aside to cool.

2. Place the chicken in a heatproof dish and steam for 25–35 minutes, or until the juices run clear when the thigh is pierced. Leave to cool. Reserve the steaming juices.

3. Chop the chicken into bite-sized pieces and arrange on a plate. Invert into a bowl and pour over the cooled stock and steaming juices. Add the two wines, tap to remove any trapped air pockets, cover and chill in the fridge overnight.

4. To remove the chicken from the bowl, dip it into a pan of hot water until the jelly around the inner surface has melted, then turn out onto a plate. Decorate the edge with coriander leaves and drizzle over some sesame oil. Serve cold.

Measurements	Ingredients
2 oz	Pork rind (finely diced)
1 pint	Chicken stock (clear)
2 slices	Ginger (crushed)
1	Spring onion (crushed)
$\frac{1}{2}$ tsp	Sugar
2 tsp	Salt
$\frac{1}{8}$ tsp	Ground white pepper
$1\frac{1}{2}$ lb	Chicken
3 tbsp	Shao Xing wine
3 tbsp	Hua Diao wine *or*
3 tbsp	Rose liqueur (if Hua Diao not available)
	Coriander leaves for garnish
	Sesame oil

Roasting and Baking

10

Barbecued Pork (1)

Measurements	Ingredients
1 lb strip	Pork loin/fillet/neck end
1 clove	Garlic, crushed
$\frac{1}{2}$ inch	Ginger (finely chopped)
2 tbsp	Rose liqueur
2 tbsp	Light soy sauce
$1\frac{1}{2}$ tbsp	Sugar
Pinch	Red food colouring
$\frac{1}{4}$ tsp	Salt.
Glaze	**Ingredients**
1 tbsp	Maltose mixed with
1 tbsp	Boiling water

Method

1. Combine all the ingredients except the glaze, cover and marinate the pork for 2–3 hours or overnight if possible.

2. Thread the pork onto a meat hook or roast pork hook/skewers and hang from the top of the oven. Roast at gas mark 7 or 190°C for 25–35 minutes.

3. Remove the pork from the oven and glaze with the maltose/water mix while still hot. Leave to cool, and glaze again if necessary. It should look glossy.

4. To serve, slice thinly on the diagonal and arrange into a large fan design. Hoisin sauce and plum sauce can be used as dipping accompaniments.

Barbecued Pork (2)

Method

1. The method for this barbecued pork dish is the same as for (1), but at stage 2, before roasting, hang up the pork to air for 45 minutes to 1 hour or until touch dry, then proceed.

Measurements	Ingredients
1lb strip	Pork loin/fillet/neck end
1½ tsp	Sugar
1 tsp	Salt
2 fl oz	Light soy sauce
1 tsp	Rose liqueur
1 tsp	Ginger juice
Pinch	Red food colouring
Glaze	Ingredients
1 tbsp	Maltose mixed with
1 tbsp	Boiling water

Barbecued Pork (3)

Method

1. Combine all the ingredients and marinate for 2–3 hours or overnight if possible.

2. Thread the pork onto a hook or skewer and roast hanging in an oven at 190° C for 25–35 minutes.

3. Glaze while hot with the maltose/water mix and leave to cool. Slice and serve as before.

Measurements	Ingredients
1 lb strip	Pork loin/fillet/neck end
1 tsp	Rose liqueur
1 tsp	Oyster sauce
1 tbsp	Braising sauce (see page 60) or
1 tsp each of	Hoisin sauce, crushed yellow bean sauce, mashed red bean curd
½ tsp	Sesame paste
1 tsp	Salt
⅛ tsp	Five-spice powder
2 tbsp	Sugar
⅛ tsp	Sand ginger powder
1½ tsp	Light soy sauce
Glaze	Ingredients
1 tbsp	Maltose mixed with
1 tbsp	Boiling water

Fish Baked (or BBQ'ed) in Salt

Method

1. De-scale the fish. Make a 1 inch (2.5cm) long cut from the tail-end of the fish towards its head.

2. Release the gills from the head, twist the gills around several times, then slowly pull them out. The entrails should follow. This will leave a cavity for stuffing.

3. Wash the cavity thoroughly. Use the back of a small knife to run down the backbone to remove the blood trail. Dry.

4. Mix the half teaspoon salt with the spices and stuff into the cavity. Cover and leave in the fridge for 30 minutes.

5. Heat the char-grill/BBQ. Separate the egg yolk from the white. Place the white into a bowl and beat until loose. Take the fish from the fridge and dry thoroughly.

6. Roll the fish in the egg white and then liberally coat in the salt. Immediately place onto the char-grill and cook for 5 minutes without moving the fish.

7. Carefully turn the fish and cook for a further 5 minutes. Remove onto a serving plate.

8. Pull away the skin and remove the fillets. Discard the rest. Serve with sweet soy sauce.

Measurements	Ingredients
1 small, whole (about 10–12oz)	Trout or mackerel (ungutted)
1 small	Spring onion (chopped)
$\frac{1}{2}$ small	Red chilli (chopped)
1 tbsp	Coriander (chopped)
1 tsp	Grated ginger
1 clove	Garlic (minced)
$\frac{1}{2}$ tsp	Salt
1	Egg white (beaten)
	Salt for coating

Steamed Dishes 11

Steamed Fish Fillets with Ham and Mushrooms

Measurements	Ingredients
12 oz	White fish fillets
4 oz	Bamboo shoots
4 oz	Ham
8	Chinese mushrooms (soaked and steamed for 15 minutes)
6 oz	Chinese broccoli *or* asparagus
$\frac{1}{2}$ tsp	Salt
1 tbsp	Oil
Seasoning	Ingredients
$\frac{1}{2}$ tsp	Sugar
1 tsp	Salt
$1\frac{1}{2}$ tsp	Potato starch
1 tbsp	Oil
Dash	White pepper
	Sesame oil

continued over →

Method

1. Wash fish and dry. Cut into 12–16 slices. Mix with seasoning ingredients and leave for 15 minutes. Cut the bamboo shoots and ham into 12–16 slices of the same size as the fish. Blanch the bamboo shoots in boiling water for 2 minutes and then drain. Cut the mushrooms in half.

2. Lightly brush a heatproof dish with oil and arrange the fish, ham, bamboo shoots and mushrooms alternately, in two or three rows on the plate. Mix the sauce ingredients (except the potato starch) and set aside.

3. Place the arranged fish in a steamer and steam for 8–10 minutes. Blanch the broccoli or asparagus in boiling salted water for 1 minute, remove and drain. Quickly stir-fry the vegetables for $1\frac{1}{2}$ minutes and place on a warm plate.

...continued

Sauce	Ingredients
$\frac{3}{4}$ tsp	Salt
5 fl oz	Chicken stock
$1\frac{1}{2}$ tsp	Potato starch
2 tsp	Oil
Dash	White pepper
Dash	Sesame oil

4. Place the sauce ingredients in a wok and pour in the steaming juices from the fish. Bring to the boil, taste, correct the seasoning and thicken with the potato starch.

5. Arrange the vegetables around the fish and pour over the sauce. Serve hot.

Spicy Steamed Fish

Method

1. De-scale and gut the fish, make 3–4 incisions on each side of the fish, and rub with the salt and pepper. Set aside for 15 minutes.

2. Combine the chillies, garlic, ginger, black beans, wine, soy sauce and potato starch and mix well.

3. Place half the spring onions on the bottom of the plate and place the fish on top. Pour over the rest of the sauce and steam over a high heat for 10–12 minutes.

4. Place the remaining spring onions over the fish. Heat the oil in a wok until smoking, pour over the spring onions and fish, garnish with some coriander and serve hot.

Measurements	Ingredients
1 whole (approx. 12–16 oz)	Fish
$\frac{1}{2}$ tsp	Salt
$\frac{1}{4}$ tsp	White pepper
2	Red chillies (sliced)
2	Green chillies (sliced)
1 clove	Garlic (chopped)
$\frac{3}{4}$ inch	Ginger (chopped)
2 tbsp	Black beans (washed)
2 tbsp	Shao Xing wine
2 tbsp	Light soy sauce
$\frac{1}{4}$ tsp	Potato starch
3	Spring onions (sliced)
4 tbsp	Oil
	Fresh coriander leaves to garnish

Eel Steamed with Black Bean Sauce

Method

1. Mix the eel rounds with the potato starch and set aside.

2. Combine all the ingredients for the black bean sauce (except the potato starch and the oils) in a bowl and, using the heel of the cleaver, grind the ingredients into a paste. Taste and correct the seasoning, add the potato starch and the oils and mix thoroughly.

3. Add half the black bean sauce to the eel and put onto a plate. Spoon over the rest of the sauce and steam for 10–12 minutes until cooked. Garnish with coriander and serve hot.

Measurements	Ingredients
1 lb	Eel (cleaned and cut into half inch thick rounds)
$\frac{1}{2}$ tsp	Potato starch
Black Bean Sauce	**Ingredients**
2 tbsp	Fermented black beans (washed)
2 cloves	Garlic (minced)
1 tsp	Ginger (minced)
$\frac{1}{2}$ tsp	Tangerine peel (chopped)
1 tsp	Red chilli (chopped)
1 tbsp	Light soy sauce
1 tsp	Shao Xing wine
2 tsp	Sugar
Dash	White pepper
Dash	Sesame oil
$\frac{1}{4}$ tsp	Potato starch
2 tsp	Vegetable oil

Fish Steamed with Spring Onions and Ginger

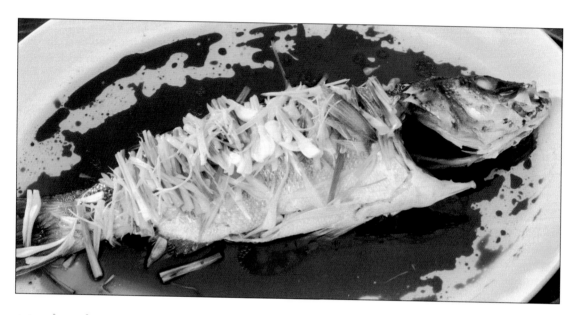

Method

1. Place the fish on a heatproof dish large enough for it to be accommodated easily. Sprinkle over a little salt and white pepper and half the shredded ginger.

2. Steam over a high heat for 10–12 minutes or until a chopstick easily penetrates the thickest part of the fish.

3. Discard the ginger that was steamed with the fish and pour off half the steaming juices if there is a lot, or all if it is discoloured.

4. Pile on the remaining ginger and the spring onions. Add a dash of sesame oil and white pepper.

5. Heat the oil until it is smoking, and pour over the ginger, spring onions and fish. Add the soy sauces and serve immediately.

Measurements	Ingredients
1 whole (approx. 1–1½ lb)	Fish (de-scaled and gutted)
	Salt
	Ground white pepper
12 slices	Ginger (shredded)

Measurements	Ingredients
4 large	Spring onions (shredded)
2 fl oz	Light soy sauce
1 tbsp	Dark soy sauce
	Ground white pepper
Dash	Sesame oil
4 fl oz	Oil

Steamed Grey Mullet/Salmon with Lemon Black Bean Sauce

Method

1. Rub the fish with the potato starch and set aside.

2. Combine all the ingredients for the black bean sauce (except the potato starch, the oils and the lemon) in a bowl and, using the heel of the cleaver, grind the ingredients into a paste. Add the lemon, taste and correct the seasoning, and add the potato starch and the oils and mix thoroughly.

3. Place half the sauce on the base of the steaming dish if using the salmon steaks, or into the stomach cavity if using a whole grey mullet. Spoon over the rest of the sauce and steam on high heat for 10–15 minutes until cooked.

4. Sprinkle over the chopped spring onions and serve hot.

Measurements	Ingredients
1 small (approx. 1–1½ lb)	Grey mullet *or*
3–4 (approx. 1 lb)	Salmon steaks
½ tsp	Potato starch
2	Spring onions (cut into rounds)
Lemon black bean sauce	**Ingredients**
2 tbsp	Fermented black beans
2 cloves	Garlic (minced)
1 tsp	Ginger (chopped)
1 tsp	Red chilli (chopped)
1 tbsp	Light soy sauce
1 tsp	Shao Xing wine
2 tsp	Sugar
Dash	White pepper
Dash	Sesame oil
¼ tsp	Potato starch
2 tsp	Vegetable oil
3 thin slices, cut into 18	Lemon

Poached Fish with Ginger and Spring Onions

Method

1. De-scale and gut the fish. Wash and trim the fins if necessary.

2. Bring a pan/wok of water to the boil. Make sure the pan/wok is large enough to hold the fish comfortably, and the water is deep enough to completely cover the fish. Add the ginger, spring onion, salt and pepper to the water, followed by the fish.

3. Bring the water back up to a gentle boil, then turn down the heat so that the water is no longer boiling, but the occasional bubble breaks the surface. Gently poach the fish for 10–15 minutes or until the thickest part of the fish is easily pierced by a chopstick.

4. Carefully remove the fish from the water and place on a serving dish. Drain and remove any bits of ginger and spring onion sticking to the fish.

Measurements	Ingredients
1 medium (approx $1\frac{1}{2}$–2 lb)	Fish
$\frac{3}{4}$ inch	Ginger (crushed)
1	Spring onion (crushed)
2 tsp	Salt
$\frac{1}{2}$ tsp	White pepper
Dash	Sesame oil
	White pepper
6–8 slices	Ginger (shredded)
4–5	Spring onions (shredded)
4 fl oz	Vegetable oil
4 tbsp	Soy sauce
1 tbsp	Dark soy sauce

5. Sprinkle over some sesame oil, white pepper and pile on the shredded ginger and spring onion.

6. Heat the vegetable oil until it is smoking, and pour it over the ginger, spring onions and fish. Add the soy sauces and serve hot.

Chef's Notes

- Suitable fish are carp, sole and bass, or any firm white-fleshed fish. Oily fish tend to be fried or steamed with stronger condiments.

Steamed Quail with Chinese Liver Sausage

Method

1. Place the quail into a clean bowl; add the marinade ingredients and mix well. Leave to marinate for 3–4 hours.

Measurements	Ingredients
2	Quail (cut into 12 pieces)

2. Soak the lotus leaf in hot water until soft and pliable. Add the sliced Chinese liver sausage to the quail and turn in the marinade.

3. Pat dry the lotus leaf and place onto a heatproof plate. Pile the quail into the centre of the leaf, and then proceed to roll up the whole package like a spring roll. Make sure that the loose flap is on the bottom.

4. Steam on a high heat for 25–35 minutes. To serve, cut open at the table.

Marinade	Ingredients
$\frac{1}{4}$ tsp	Salt
$\frac{1}{2}$ tsp	Sugar
$\frac{1}{2}$ tsp	Dark soy sauce
$\frac{1}{2}$ tsp	Light soy sauce
$\frac{1}{2}$ tsp	Potato starch
$\frac{1}{2}$ tsp	Ginger (crushed)
1	Spring onion (cut into 1cm pieces)
1 tsp	Rose liqueur
Pinch	Ground white pepper
Dash	Sesame oil
1	Lotus leaf (dried)
1	Chinese liver sausage (cut into slices)

Steamed Roast Duck with Sour Plum Sauce

Method

1. Chop the duck into bite-sized pieces and arrange into an approximation of its original shape but circular. Place a heatproof bowl over the duck and invert the duck into it.

2. Prepare the sour plum sauce by first frying the ginger and garlic in a wok with the oil over a low heat until brown and sticky. Add the preserved plums. Add the chilli and tangerine peel and carry on frying until pungent, then add the water, vinegar, sugar and cook until the sugar has melted. Taste and correct the seasoning.

Measurements	Ingredients
$\frac{1}{2}$	Cantonese-style roast duck
2 tbsp	Ginger (finely chopped)
2 tbsp	Garlic (finely chopped)
1 tbsp	Oil
6–8	Preserved/sour plums (de-stoned)
1	Red chilli (chopped)
1 piece	Dried tangerine peel (soaked and chopped)
$\frac{1}{4}$ pint	Water
$\frac{1}{4}$ pint	Malt/white vinegar

continued over →

3. Pour the sauce over the duck and tap gently to release any trapped air bubbles. Cover loosely with cling film and steam over a high heat for 1–1½ hours until the duck is meltingly soft. Leave the duck to stand for 10 minutes.

4. Drain the juices off into a bowl and skim off as much of the fat as possible and discard. Pour the sauce and juices into a wok and gently bring to the boil. Taste and correct the seasoning, thicken if necessary with the potato starch and water. Add a pinch of ground white pepper and a dash of sesame oil.

5. Pour over the duck ensuring all the duck is evenly coated. Garnish with some coriander leaves and serve hot.

...continued

Measurements	Ingredients
2 oz	Yellow rock sugar
	Salt to taste
	Potato starch/water for thickening
Pinch	Ground white pepper
Dash	Sesame oil
	Coriander leaves for garnish

Scallops Steamed in the Shell with Garlic/Black Bean Sauce

Measurements	Ingredients
2	Scallops per person
1 tsp	Crushed fried garlic flakes in 1 tsp oil *or*
1 tsp	Black bean sauce per 2 scallops
1 tbsp	Spring onion, green (chopped)
Sauce	Ingredients
2	Spring onion, white (shredded)
1 tbsp	Light soy sauce
2 tsp	Oil
Dash	White pepper
Dash	Sesame oil

Method

1. Open the scallops and remove from the shell. Remove and discard the skirt, remove the coral and save for stir-frying. Remove the tough muscle on the side of the white meat and discard. Wash the white scallop meat and drain on some kitchen paper. Repeat with all the scallops.

2. Scrub the shells and then place into boiling water and boil for 5 minutes. Drain and cool under cold water. Remove and dry.

3. To make the sauce, place the shredded spring onion whites into a bowl and pour over the soy sauce, oil, white pepper and sesame oil. Set aside.

4. Place 1 scallop meat per shell, top each scallop with either half a teaspoon garlic/oil or half a teaspoon black bean sauce.

5. Sprinkle with the chopped green of the spring onion and place on a heatproof plate. Steam for 5–6 minutes. To serve, each person takes one scallop at a time, and adds a little of the sauce. Using a fork or chopstick push down on the scallop to break slightly to absorb the sauce and juices. After eating the scallop, the remaining juices are drunk straight from the shell.

Chicken Buns

Method

1. Mix the filling ingredients with the marinade ingredients and set aside.

2. To make the dough, mix the ammonium bicarbonate with 1 tablespoon water.

3. Sift the flour and baking powder together.

4. Mix the sugar, lard, vinegar and ammonium bicarbonate in a bowl. Add in three-quarters of a cup water, mix well. Add in the flour and mix. Turn out the paste and knead it well, until it is soft and smooth. Cover with a damp cloth or cling film and leave for 15 minutes. Turn out and knead again for 5 minutes, then cover and leave for a further 30 minutes.

Dough	Ingredients
$\frac{1}{4}$ tsp	Ammonium bicarbonate
14 oz	Plain soft flour
$2\frac{1}{2}$ tsp	Baking powder
$\frac{2}{3}$ cup	Sugar
$\frac{3}{4}$ tbsp	Lard
$\frac{1}{2}$ tsp	White vinegar
Some 2 inch (5cm)	Square pieces of greaseproof paper
Filling	Ingredients
12 oz	Chicken (roughly chopped)
1	Chinese liver sausage (chopped)
4	Chinese mushrooms (soaked and diced)

continued over →

5. Divide the mixture into 10–12 pieces and roll into a ball. Flatten out into rounds of about 6mm thickness. Place a portion of the filling into the centre and draw up the sides into a bun shape. Place the buns onto a square of paper and place onto a heatproof plate. Steam over a high heat for 12–15 minutes.

6. Omitting the chicken, you can make mantow, plain steamed northern bread.

Chef's Notes

- The ammonium bicarbonate must be fully dissolved in the water or it will have an unpleasant odour.

...continued

2 oz	Bamboo shoots (blanched and shredded)
1 tbsp	Coriander (roughly chopped)
Marinade	**Ingredients**
$\frac{3}{4}$ tsp	Salt
$\frac{1}{2}$ tsp	Sugar
2 tsp	Potato starch
1 tbsp	Oil
Dash	Sesame oil
	Ground white pepper

Barbecued Pork Buns

Method

1. Prepare the filling by first frying the ginger and spring onion in the oil. Add in all the seasoning ingredients except the thickening and bring to the boil. Stir in the thickening and add the pork. Mix well and set aside to cool.

2. To make the dough sift the baking powder and the flour together.

3. Add 1 tablespoon water to the ammonium bicarbonate and mix well.

4. Place the sugar, vinegar, lard and ammonium bicarbonate in a bowl and mix well. Add the water and mix. Add in the flour and mix well. Turn out onto a table and knead until soft and smooth. Cover with a damp cloth and leave for 15 minutes. Turn out and knead again for 5 minutes, then cover and leave for a further 30 minutes.

Dough	Ingredients
$2\frac{1}{2}$ tsp	Baking powder
14 oz	Flour
$\frac{1}{4}$ tsp	Ammonium bicarbonate
$\frac{2}{3}$ cup	Sugar
$\frac{1}{2}$ tsp	White vinegar
$\frac{3}{4}$ tsp	Lard
$\frac{3}{4}$ cup	Water
Some 2 inch (5cm)	Square pieces of greaseproof paper
Filling	**Ingredients**
8 oz	Barbecued pork (diced)
1 slice	Ginger (chopped)
1	Spring onion (chopped)
1 tbsp	Oil

5. Divide the dough into 10–12 pieces and roll into balls. Flatten out into 6mm thick rounds and place some filling into the centre. Draw up the side to seal the filling into a bun shape. Place onto a piece of greaseproof paper and steam over a high heat for 10–12 minutes.

Seasoning	Ingredients
$\frac{3}{4}$ tsp	Sesame oil
$1\frac{1}{2}$ tbsp	Oyster sauce
1 tsp	Light soy sauce
$\frac{3}{4}$ tsp	Dark soy sauce
$2\frac{1}{2}$ tbsp	Sugar
$\frac{1}{2}$ cup	Water
Dash	White pepper
$1\frac{1}{2}$ tbsp	Water chestnut powder mixed with
4 tbsp	Water to thicken

Shrimp Dumplings

Method

1. Dice the shrimps, then crush and finely chop half of them. Place into a bowl.

2. In a dry wok, gently fry the bamboo shoots until excess liquid is gone. Cool and place in the bowl with the shrimps. Add the pork back fat and the seasonings and mix well until sticky. This is the filling.

3. To make the dough, bring the water to the boil and turn down to the lowest heat. Add in the wheat starch and mix quickly. Remove the pot from the stove and cover with a cloth for 5 minutes.

4. Turn out the hot dough onto a surface dusted with wheat starch, add the oil and knead until smooth and soft. Wrap in oiled cling film and allow to reach room temperature.

5. Roll the dough out into a large thin sheet, and using a cutter (2 inches wide), cut discs from the sheet. Re-knead and reuse the leftovers until you get about 16–18 discs. If the discs are too thick they can be individually re-rolled into thinner discs.

Filling	Ingredients
8 oz	Shrimps (peeled and de-veined)
$1\frac{1}{2}$ oz	Bamboo shoots (blanched and diced)
2 tbsp	Pork back fat (finely diced)
Seasoning	**Ingredients**
$\frac{1}{2}$ tsp	Salt
$\frac{1}{4}$ tsp	Sugar
1 tbsp	Potato starch
$\frac{1}{2}$ tbsp	Oil
Dash	Sesame oil
	White pepper
Dough	**Ingredients**
6 oz	Wheat starch
$1\frac{1}{3}$ cups	Water
$\frac{1}{2}$ tbsp	Oil

6. Pleat one side of the pastry discs to form 12 folds; add some of the filling and seal shut with firm pinches to form a semi-crescent at the front. Place onto an oiled steel dim sum disc in a bamboo steamer or a heatproof plate, and steam for 8 minutes.

Chef's Notes

- The flour should be put into the water, not the other way round. If the starch is not fully cooked and elastic, it will split when steamed.

Scallop Dumplings

Method

1. To make the filling, quickly blanch the scallops in boiling water for 30 seconds. Remove, drain and cut into $\frac{1}{4}$ inch dice. Dry-fry the black pepper and add to the scallops along with the crushed garlic flakes, carrot, water chestnuts and the seasoning ingredients and mix well. Set aside.

2. To make the dough sift the wheat starch and the cornflour together. Bring the water to the boil, turn down to the lowest heat and add the wheat starch and cornflour. Stir in quickly, cover and leave for 5 minutes. Turn out onto a table and knead in the potato starch while still hot. Add the oil and knead until soft, smooth and elastic.

3. Roll out the dough into a thin sheet. Use a 2-inch round cutter to cut out discs. Re-knead and re-use the trimmings.

4. Place some filling into the centre of the discs and fold into a tricorn shape. Repeat with the remaining discs. Place onto an oiled plate and steam for 8 minutes.

Filling	Ingredients
$10\frac{2}{3}$ oz	Scallops
$\frac{1}{2}$ tsp	Ground black pepper
1 tbsp	Fried garlic flakes (crushed)
2 oz	Carrot (cooked and diced)
4	Water chestnuts (diced)
Seasoning	Ingredients
$\frac{1}{2}$ tsp	Salt
1 tbsp	Potato starch
Dash	Sesame oil
Dough	Ingredients
$5\frac{1}{3}$ oz	Wheat starch
$2\frac{1}{2}$ tbsp	Cornflour
$1\frac{1}{2}$ cups	Water
$2\frac{1}{2}$ tbsp	Potato starch
$\frac{1}{2}$ tbsp	Oil

Chef's Notes

- The ratio of flour to water is very important. When boiling the water, keep an eye on it otherwise the water will dry up and the ratio will change.

Pork and Prawn Dumplings (Siu Mai)

Method

1. To make the filling, dice the prawns, and crush and finely chop one-third of them. Place into a bowl. Finely dice the pork, then take one-quarter of the pork and crush. Place into the bowl with the prawns.

2. Add the seasoning ingredients and stir until sticky.

3. Place some filling onto the wonton wrappers and form into free-standing, open-topped, short cylinders, making sure that the filling sticks to the pastry.

4. Place onto an oiled plate or steamer and steam for 8–10 minutes until cooked.

Chef's Notes

- These dumplings look better with some crab roe on top, but this is hard to come by, so artificial crab roe can be used.

- Artificial crab roe: 1tbsp flour, pinch red or orange food colouring and 1tbsp water. Mix well and steam for 5 minutes. Chop into little pieces and add to the raw dumplings.

Measurements	Ingredients
11 oz	Pork chop *or*
8 oz	Pork fillet
3 oz	Pork back fat
5 oz	Prawns, peeled
25	Wonton wrappers (round)
Seasoning	**Ingredients**
$\frac{1}{2}$ tsp	Salt
$\frac{1}{2}$ tsp	Sugar
$\frac{1}{2}$ tsp	Shao Xing wine
$\frac{1}{2}$ tsp	Oyster sauce
$\frac{1}{2}$ tbsp	Light soy sauce
1	Egg white
1 tbsp	Potato starch
Dash	Sesame oil
	White pepper

Steamed Shrimp Crescents

Method

1. De-vein the shrimps, then dice and crush one-third of them. Place into a bowl. Add the prepared bamboo shoots, coriander, pork back fat and seasonings. Mix well.

2. To make the dough sift the wheat starch and cornflour into a bowl. Bring the water to the boil, turn down the heat to its lowest setting and add the wheat starch and cornflour. Mix in quickly and cover with a cloth for 5 minutes.

Dough	Ingredients
$5\frac{1}{3}$ oz	Wheat starch
$2\frac{1}{2}$ tbsp	Cornflour
$1\frac{1}{2}$ cups	Water
$2\frac{1}{2}$ tbsp	Potato starch
$\frac{1}{2}$ tbsp	Oil

continued over →

...continued

3. Turn the hot dough out onto a table and knead in the potato starch. Add the oil and knead until soft, smooth and elastic.

4. Roll out the dough into a thin sheet and cut out $2\frac{1}{2}$ inch diameter discs using a cutter. Place some of the filling into the centre of the discs and fold in half to form half moons. Seal the ends tightly.

5. Place onto an oiled plate and steam for 8 minutes until done.

Filling	Ingredients
8 oz	Shrimps (peeled)
2 oz	Bamboo shoots (blanched, shredded and pan dried)
2 stalks	Coriander (minced)
2 tbsp	Cooked pork back fat (finely diced)
Seasoning	Ingredients
$\frac{1}{2}$ tsp	Salt
$\frac{1}{4}$ tsp	Sugar
1 tbsp	Potato starch
$\frac{1}{2}$ tbsp	Oil
Dash	Sesame oil
	White pepper

Turnip Pudding

Method

1. In a wok, gently fry the diced sausages and preserved pork until the fat oozes out and the meats are nicely caramelised. Remove the meat to a bowl. Fry the shrimps in the fat until fragrant and remove to the bowl.

2. Add the oil to the wok and add the grated turnip, including the liquid, and the wine. Add the sugar and white pepper and cook until transparent. Add the mushroom soaking liquid and shrimp liquid as required. Add the salt and the mushrooms, fried meats and shrimps. Taste and correct seasoning.

3. Turn down the heat to its lowest setting and add the rice flour and potato starch by the spoonful, stirring all the time. If the mixture

Measurements	Ingredients
1	Chinese pork sausage (diced)
1	Chinese liver sausage (diced)
2 oz	Preserved pork belly (diced)
1 oz	Dried shrimps (soaked)
1 tbsp	Oil
1 tsp	Shao Xing wine
20 oz	White radish (peeled and grated)
1 tbsp	Sugar

looks too sloppy, add more rice flour and starch until it resembles thick porridge.

4. Turn the mixture into an oiled cake tin and steam over a high heat for 30–45 minutes. Test if the pudding is cooked by inserting a skewer: if it comes out clean, the pudding is done, if not, steam for a further 10 minutes and test again.

5. Sprinkle the sesame seeds and the coriander on top and leave to stand for 10 minutes before serving. To serve, cut into quarters and then cut the quarters into thick slices. This pudding can be left overnight and then sliced and fried as a breakfast or lunch dish. Serve with chilli oil or chilli sauce.

Measurements	Ingredients
$\frac{1}{4}$ tsp	White pepper
4	Chinese mushrooms (soaked and diced)
1 tsp	Salt
4 oz	Rice flour
2 tsp	Potato starch dissolved in 2 tbsp water
1 tbsp	White sesame seeds (roasted)
1 handful	Coriander leaves (torn)

Taro Pudding

Method

1. Put the taro in a steamer and steam for 30 minutes. Remove from the steamer, cool and then dice.

2. Gently fry the sausages and pork until the fat oozes out. Add the oil and wine and then the shrimps and stir for about 1 minute until fragrant. Scoop out and place in a bowl.

3. Place the rice flour in the middle of a large bowl and form a well. Gradually add the cold water, drawing in the rice flour with your hands. Add the taro and stir to mix. Add the salt, pepper and five-spice powder and mix. Add all but two tablespoons of the meat and shrimp and mix thoroughly.

4. Pour everything into an oiled heatproof dish. Put the dish into the steamer and steam on a high heat for 15 minutes. Remove from the steamer and using a pair of chopsticks, stir and turn the mixture thoroughly. Some of the taro will

Measurements	Ingredients
10 oz	Taro (peeled and cut into 1 inch (2.5cm) thick slices)
1	Chinese pork sausage (diced)
1	Chinese liver sausage (diced)
2 oz	Preserved pork belly (diced)
1 tbsp	Oil
1 tsp	Shao Xing wine
1 oz	Dried shrimp (soaked and chopped)
4 oz	Rice flour
8 fl oz	Water
$\frac{1}{2}$ tsp	Salt

continued over →

become mushy so use a palette knife or spoon to smooth the surface. Scatter over the remaining meat and shrimp and continue to steam for a further 30–45 minutes.

5. Test the pudding with a skewer to see if it is cooked. If it is cooked, remove and sprinkle on the sesame seeds, coriander leaves and chilli rounds. Let the dish stand before serving. To serve, cut into quarters and then slices. This dish can be left overnight and then sliced and fried for breakfast or lunch. Serve with soy sauce or chilli oil.

...continued

Measurements	Ingredients
$\frac{1}{4}$ tsp	White pepper
$\frac{1}{4}$ tsp	Five-spice powder
1 tbsp	White sesame seeds (roasted)
1 handful	Coriander leaves
	Deseeded red chilli rounds for garnish

Steamed Chicken with Chinese Sausage in Lotus Leaf

Measurements	Ingredients
1	Dried lotus leaf
1	Chinese liver sausage
1	Chinese pork sausage
8–10	Chinese mushrooms (tinned)
2	Spring onions
10 oz	Prepared chicken in steaming marinade (see page 61)
2 tbsp	Oil for frying

Method

1. Soak the dried lotus leaf in boiling water for 10 minutes.

2. Slice the Chinese sausages on the diagonal into 10–12 slices. Fry in a dry wok until fragrant and caramelised. Drain on kitchen paper.

3. Cut the mushrooms in half if they are too large.

4. Cut the spring onion whites on the diagonal into thick slices. Chop the greens and save for garnish.

5. Quickly fry the chicken in the hot oil in a wok for 2 minutes, but do not colour. This is to prevent the chicken from sticking together when wrapped and steamed.

6. Place the prepared chicken, mushrooms, sausages and spring onion whites into a bowl and mix well.

7. Remove the lotus leaf from the water and pat dry. Place into a bowl and pile in the chicken. Wrap up and place onto a plate. Steam for 30–40 minutes.

8. To serve, cut open in front of the guests and sprinkle over the reserved chopped spring onion greens.

Steamed Scallops with Ham and Mushrooms

Method

1. Cut the scallop meat three-quarters of the way through and place a square of ham in the centre. Place onto a lightly oiled plate.

2. Place the mushrooms into a bowl and cover with cling film. Place into a steamer along with the scallop and steam for 5 minutes.

3. While the mushrooms and scallops are steaming, bring a wok of water to the boil. Add the salt and oil. Poach the asparagus for 4–5 minutes until just cooked. Drain and place in a row on a warm plate.

4. Remove the scallops when they are just opaque and firm to the touch. Remove the mushrooms also, and arrange alternately with the scallops to form three rows.

5. Place the steaming juices along with the ham stock into a wok and bring to the boil. Season to taste and thicken slightly to form a thin glaze. Add a dash of sesame oil and carefully dress over the scallops, mushrooms and asparagus.

Measurements	Ingredients
12	Fresh scallop meat
12 slices (approx. 1 inch square)	Cooked Chinese ham
12	Chinese mushrooms, braised (flower type preferable)
1 tbsp	Salt
4 tbsp	Oil
1 bunch	Asparagus (trimmed and cut into 4 inch lengths)
4 fl oz	Ham stock
	Salt and white pepper to taste
	Potato starch and water to thicken
Dash	Sesame oil

Ribs Steamed in Black Bean Sauce

Method

1. Chop the ribs into $\frac{1}{2}$ inch pieces. Rinse to remove any bone fragments and pat dry. Place into a large bowl.

2. Add the potato starch and work it into the ribs. Add the salt, sugar, soy sauce, white pepper, garlic, chilli and the preserved/pickled plums, and thoroughly mix with the ribs.

3. Add the vegetable oil and gently turn into the ribs.

4. Wash the black beans in a bowl to remove excess salt and drain on some kitchen paper. Add the beans to the ribs and mix carefully so as not to break up the beans. Add a good dash of sesame oil and leave to marinate for 3–4 hours or overnight if possible.

5. Put ribs onto a heatproof plate and steam for 20 minutes. Serve hot.

Measurements	Ingredients
1 lb	Pork ribs
2 tsp	Potato starch
$\frac{3}{4}$ tsp	Salt
2 tsp	Sugar
1 tsp	Light soy sauce
Pinch	White pepper
3 cloves	Garlic (finely chopped)
1	Red chilli (deseeded and sliced into rounds)
2	Preserved/pickled plums (stones removed)
1 tbsp	Vegetable oil
$\frac{1}{2}$ tbsp	Black beans
Dash	Sesame oil

Mushrooms/Asparagus Stuffed with Prawn Paste

Method

1. Brush off any dirt on the mushrooms and trim off the stem. Cut the woody stem off the asparagus and then trim them all to the same length. Peel the stems leaving the bud intact.

2. Blanch the asparagus in boiling salted water for 1 minute, then refresh. Drain and cover with damp cloth or cling film to prevent drying.

3. Place all the ingredients for the poaching liquor into a pan and bring to a boil. Turn down the heat to a simmer and add the mushrooms. Cook for 1 minute only or until they soften. Remove and drain thoroughly on kitchen paper.

Measurements	Ingredients
12	Fresh shiitake mushrooms, of even size
6 spears	Fresh asparagus
8–10 oz	Prawn paste
Poaching liquor	**Ingredients**
16 fl oz	Plain chicken stock
$\frac{1}{2}$ tsp	Salt
$\frac{1}{2}$ tsp	Sugar
1 tbsp	Oyster sauce
Pinch	White pepper

4. Lightly dab the inside of the mushrooms and the stems of the asparagus with a little potato starch. Fill the mushrooms with the prawn paste, taking care to smooth them off. Brush the prawn paste with a little oil to prevent drying.

5. Wrap the prawn paste around the stems of the asparagus by first forming the paste into balls, and then pushing the stems through. Smooth out the paste so that it covers half the stem. A little egg white on your hands will prevent sticking.

To finish	Ingredients
	Plain chicken stock
	Salt, white pepper to taste
	Potato starch to thicken
1 tbsp	Egg white, beaten
Dash	Sesame oil

6. Place onto a lightly oiled plate and cover loosely with foil. Steam for 7–8 minutes.

7. Pour off the steaming juices into a pan and add enough stock to make 4 fluid ounces. Bring to a gentle simmer. Taste and correct the seasoning. Thicken to a light syrup consistency. Turn off the heat and gently stir in the egg white. Spoon over the mushrooms and asparagus.

Seafood Siu Mai

Method

1. Combine all the seafood in a bowl and add the seasoning.

2. Stir in one direction until the mixture is quite firm.

3. Remove the corners from the won ton wrappers.

4. Place one-sixth of the filling into the centre of the wonton wrapper.

5. Draw up the sides of the wrapper around the filling, adding extra as required, to form an open-topped dumpling. The sides should be straight, resembling a short cylinder.

6. Garnish with a small piece of crab roe.

7. Place into a bamboo steamer, and steam for 6–8 minutes. Serve with soy sauce and chilli and ginger sauce.

Measurements	Ingredients
2 oz	Tiger prawns (half chopped, half mashed)
1 large	Fresh scallop (diced)
1 oz	Fresh white crab meat (cooked)
1 large	Langoustine tail (diced)
1 oz	Dover sole fillet (diced)
	Cooked crab roe for garnish
6	Won ton wrappers
Seasoning	Ingredients
1 tsp	Ginger juice
Large pinch	Salt
2 large pinches	Sugar
Pinch	Ground white pepper
1 tsp	Chives (chopped)
Dash	Sesame oil
$\frac{1}{4}$ tsp	Potato starch

Mushroom with Crab

Method

1. Steam or poach the fresh shiitake mushrooms in lightly seasoned stock for 2–3 minutes, or steam braised shiitake mushrooms until hot. Drain.

2. Place stock and fried garlic into a wok and gently heat until simmering, season the stock and add the wine. Simmer for 1 minute. Remove the garlic.

3. Thicken the stock to a light consistency, and add the crab and warm through. Taste and correct the seasoning.

4. Turn off the heat and gently dribble in the egg white while slowly stirring, to form thin egg flowers. Add a dash of sesame oil.

5. Place the mushrooms, cap upwards, onto a warm plate and border with the greens. Dress the sauce evenly over the mushrooms.

6. Garnish with crab coral in a little pile in the centre.

Chef's Notes

- Deep-fried cooked Chinese ham is an alternative to the coral.

- Do not thicken the sauce too much as the egg white will thicken the sauce further.

Measurements	Ingredients
12 1 tin 10 oz	Shiitake mushrooms, fresh or braised or Straw mushrooms or Mixed mushrooms
8 fl oz	Chicken stock or Chicken and ham stock
1 clove	Garlic (crushed and lightly fried until golden, then drained)
1 tsp	Shao Xing wine
	Potato starch and water for thickening
4–5 oz	White crab meat in large pieces
1	Egg white (beaten)
Dash	Sesame oil
6oz	Blanched green leaf vegetables to border plate and mushrooms
1 tbsp	Cooked, chopped crab coral for garnish if available
	Salt and white pepper for seasoning

Crab with Asparagus

Method

1. Quickly blanch the asparagus in boiling lightly salted water (30 seconds) to which half the oil has been added. Drain and refresh.

2. In a wok, add the remaining oil and the shredded ginger. Fry lightly without colouring the ginger. Drain off the oil and add the stock.

3. Bring to a gentle simmer, add the dark soy sauce, oyster sauce and season with salt and white pepper.

4. Thicken to a light consistency and add the asparagus and crab leg meat. Warm through, taking care not to break up the crab.

5. Turn off the heat and add dash of sesame oil.

6. To serve, place the asparagus onto a plate in two rows, one of tips and the other of stems, approximating spears of asparagus. Place the crab leg meat neatly on top of the asparagus, and pour over the remaining sauce.

7. Garnish with a sprinkle of the deep-fried Chinese ham shreds.

Measurements	Ingredients
1 bunch	Asparagus (peeled and cut into equal lengths)
2 tbsp	Oil
3 slices	Ginger (shredded)
6 fl oz	Stock
2 drops	Dark soy sauce
1 tsp	Oyster sauce
	Potato starch and water to thicken
6 oz	Whole crab leg meat
Dash	Sesame oil
	Deep-fried shredded Chinese ham for garnish
	Salt and white pepper to season

Deep-fried Dishes 12

Sweet and Sour Fish

Measurements	Ingredients
1 lb	White fish fillets (cut into slices)
2 tsp	Potato starch
$\frac{3}{4}$ tsp	Salt
$\frac{1}{4}$ tsp	White pepper
1	Egg white
Sweet and Sour sauce	**Ingredients**
10 fl oz	White malt vinegar
1 fl oz	Worcester sauce
6 oz	Slice sugar
	Salt to taste
2 oz	Tomato ketchup
$\frac{1}{2}$	Lemon (juice only)
2 oz	Carrot/onion (shredded)
1 tbsp	Oil
2 oz	Pineapple (cut into quarters)
$1\frac{1}{2}$ tsp	Potato starch in 4 tbsp water
	Sesame oil

Method

1. Mix the sliced fillet of white fish with the potato starch, salt, white pepper and the egg white and set aside for 30 minutes.

2. Combine all the ingredients for the sweet and sour sauce (except the vegetables and potato starch mixture) and bring to the boil. Taste and correct the seasoning, thicken slightly and put to one side.

3. Dredge the fish in potato starch and deep-fry in very hot oil for 3–4 minutes until golden and very crispy. Drain on kitchen paper and put onto a serving dish.

4. Fry the carrot and onion shreds in the oil, add the sweet and sour sauce and the pineapple bits and bring to the boil. Taste and correct the seasoning and the consistency if required. Add a dash of sesame oil, pour over the fish and serve hot.

Deep-fried Eel with Spiced Salt, Chilli, Garlic and Coriander

Method

1. Slice the eel fillet on the slant into 12–16 pieces, then add the five-spice powder, salt, potato starch and white pepper. Mix thoroughly then add the egg white. Mix until sticky, then press each piece of eel into potato starch until evenly coated.

2. To make the spiced salt, heat the salt in a saucepan until lightly coloured, remove from the heat and then add the ground Sichuan peppercorns. Leave to cool. Store in a jar and use as required.

3. Heat a wok half full of oil to 190° C and deep-fry the eel for 3–4 minutes until light golden and crunchy. Drain on kitchen paper and keep warm.

4. In a wok gently fry the chilli and white peppercorns in the oil until pungent. Add the eel and the garlic flakes and turn the pieces of eel to coat them. Sprinkle over the spiced salt and sugar evenly, add the coriander and spring onion, toss over a high heat until the coriander has wilted. Add a dash of sesame oil and serve hot.

Measurements	Ingredients
1 (approx. 1–1½ lb)	Eel fillet
Pinch	Five-spice powder
1 tsp	Salt
1 tsp	Potato starch
¼ tsp	White pepper
1	Egg white
	Potato starch for dredging
	Spiced salt to taste (see below)
	Vegetable oil for deep-frying
1	Red chilli (sliced)
1 tsp	Crushed white peppercorns
1 tsp	Oil
2 tsp	Fried garlic flakes (crushed)
¼ tsp	Sugar
3 handfuls	Coriander (roughly chopped)
1	Spring onion (chopped)
Dash	Sesame oil
Spiced Salt	**Ingredients**
2 tbsp	Salt
¼ tsp	Ground Sichuan peppercorns

Deep-fried Squid with Spiced Salt

Method

1. To prepare the fresh squid, pull the head away from the body of the squid. Cut away the tentacles just in front of the eyes. Using a tissue, draw off as much of the pink/purple skin as possible. Wash and place in a bowl.

2. Feel inside the cavity of the squid and draw out the quill, a transparent sheath, and discard. Using a pair of scissors, cut along the natural seam to open up the squid. Discard the innards and remove all the pink/purple skin. Remove the fins and the skin and wash and dry.

3. Take the squid and place it skinned side down, horizontally, pointed end left or right. Take a sharp knife and score vertically along the length of the squid.

Measurements	Ingredients
1 whole (approx. 1 lb)	Squid
1	Egg white
$\frac{1}{4}$ tsp	Five-spice powder
Pinch	Ground white pepper
	Potato starch for dredging
	Oil for deep-frying
$\frac{1}{2}$ tsp	Spiced salt (see page 54)
	Lemon wedges for serving
	Parsley sprigs
	Worcester sauce for dipping

4. Turn the squid through 90 degrees so that the pointed end is facing up or down. Taking a sharp knife, make diagonal cuts at a shallow angle (10 degrees to the horizontal), but do not cut through. Make two shallow cuts (scores), then cut through on the third pass. The strips should be about 1.5cm wide and about 8cm long. Repeat for all the squid, fins included.

5. Cut the squid into bite-sized pieces. Pat dry and place into a bowl. The tentacles should be cut into pairs or left whole to use as a focal point when serving.

6. Add the egg white, five-spice powder and white pepper to the squid. Mix thoroughly and leave for 30 minutes.

7. Dredge the pieces of squid in the potato starch and set aside. Heat a wok one-third full of oil to a very high temperature (just beginning to smoke). Carefully add the squid and fry for only 30–40 seconds. Remove and drain.

8. To serve, place onto a serving dish, sprinkle with the spiced salt, garnish with the lemon wedges and parsley sprigs and accompany with the Worcester sauce.

Oysters in Batter

Method

1. Bring a wok of water to boil. Add the oysters and poach for 15 seconds, just to set the outside. Remove and drain on kitchen paper. Sprinkle lightly with five-spice powder and white pepper.

2. To make the batter, place the flour in a bowl and add a pinch of salt. Add enough water to form a thick pancake-consistency batter. Do not overmix as the resulting batter will be tough. Leave to rest for 30 minutes.

3. Bring a wok half full of oil to 180–190° C. Dip the oysters into plain or self-raising flour then into the batter. Let the excess batter run off, then deep-fry the oysters for 3–4 minutes, holding them under the oil with a spider once the outside has set.

4. Remove the oysters and drain on kitchen paper. Repeat until all are done. The oysters should be crisp on the outside and juicy on the inside. Serve garnished with lemon, with spiced salt and Worcester sauce for dipping.

Measurements	Ingredients
10 oz	Oyster meat
	Five-spice powder
	White pepper
	Oil for deep-frying
	Lemon wedges to garnish
	Spiced salt (see page 54)
	Worcester sauce for dipping
Batter	**Ingredients**
4 oz	Self-raising flour
Pinch	Salt
	Water

Deep-fried Dumplings

Measurements	Ingredients
18	Dumpling wrappers
Filling	**Ingredients**
8 oz	Lean pork
1½ oz	Dried shrimps
4	Chinese mushrooms
4	Water chestnuts
3 tbsp	Oil
1 tsp	Ginger juice
1 tsp	Wine

continued over →

Method

1. Mince the pork. Soak the dried shrimps until soft, then dice. Soak the mushrooms and dice along with the water chestnuts.

2. To make the filling, fry the shrimps in a wok with 2 tablespoons oil. Add the ginger juice and wine, stir and remove to a bowl. Add the remaining oil to the wok then add the pork, mushrooms and water chestnuts. Stir-fry for 2 minutes then add the shrimps. Add the seasoning and cook until the sauce almost dries up. Add the thickening ingredients, place into a bowl and allow to cool.

...continued

1 tsp	Potato starch mixed with 2 tbsp water for thickening
Seasoning	**Ingredients**
$\frac{1}{2}$ tsp	Salt
2 tsp	Light soy sauce
$\frac{1}{3}$ tsp	Sugar
3 tbsp	Water
Dash	Sesame oil and white pepper

3. Place $1\frac{1}{2}$ teaspoons of the cooled filling into the centre of each wrapper. Pleat one side of the wrapper and seal to form a crescent.

4. Deep-fry the crescents in hot oil (170–180° C) for 3–4 minutes until golden. Drain and serve with chilli oil.

Sesame Prawn Toast

Method

1. Cut the crusts off the slices of bread and place to one side.

2. Using a dinner knife spread the prawn paste evenly over the bread in a thin 2–3mm layer.

3. Dip the prawn side down into a plate of sesame seeds and press firmly to ensure good adhesion. Shake off the excess seeds. Repeat with the other three slices.

4. Heat a wok one-third full of oil to 160–170° C. Test with a small cube of bread. If it sizzles immediately on contact and browns in 30–45 seconds then the oil is ready.

5. Place the slices of prawn bread into the oil, sesame seed side down, and deep-fry for 45–60 seconds.

6. Turn over and deep-fry the other side for 30–45 seconds until golden brown. Drain on kitchen paper. Cut in triangles, fingers or squares and serve hot.

Measurements	Ingredients
4 slices	Fresh white bread
6 oz	Prawn paste
	White sesame seeds to coat
	Oil for deep-frying

Chef's Notes

• Fresh bread is used rather than stale as it has a higher moisture content and will absorb less oil than stale.

• The prawn paste must be in a thin layer otherwise it will not cook before the sesame seeds are golden.

Phoenix Rolls

Method

1. Remove the crusts and roll the bread flat with a rolling pin.

2. Spread the bread with the prawn paste, leaving a $\frac{3}{4}$ inch gap at one end.

3. Trim the quartered sausage so that it fits the width of the bread and place one quarter on the end of each piece of bread on top of the prawn paste.

4. Place a line of coriander leaves in front of the sausage.

5. Brush the end of the uncovered bread with some egg yolk and roll up. Roll firmly at the end to ensure good adhesion.

Measurements	Ingredients
4 slices	Fresh white bread
4–5 oz	Prawn paste
1	Chinese pork sausage (cooked and quartered lengthwise)
	Coriander leaves
1	Egg yolk
	Oil for deep-frying

6. Heat a wok one-third full of oil to 150–160°C and gently fry the rolls for 2–3 minutes until golden and crisp. Remove and drain on kitchen paper.

7. Serve either by cutting into rounds or slicing each into half on the diagonal. Serve with Worcester sauce.

Wun Nam Prawns

Method

1. Combine all the ingredients and leave for 15–20 minutes.

2. Dredge in potato starch and shake off excess.

3. Heat a wok one-third full of oil to a high heat 180–190°C.

4. Deep-fry for 30–40 seconds and remove and drain. Serve with lemon wedges and Worcester sauce.

Measurements	Ingredients
12	King prawns (shelled and de-veined)
½ cube	Fermented red beancurd
2 tbsp	Fermented red beancurd juice
Large pinch	Five-spice powder
1 tsp	Rose liqueur
1 tsp	Sugar
Large pinch	White pepper
2 cloves	Garlic (minced)
Good dash	Sesame oil
	Potato starch for dredging
	Oil for deep-frying
	Lemon wedges
	Worcester sauce

Spring Rolls

Method

1. Heat the oil in a wok until smoking. Add the vegetables and the meat and fry for 3–4 minutes until hot and cooked. Add the seasonings. Taste and correct the seasoning. Add the pepper and the sesame oil.

2. Scoop the filling into a colander and allow to cool and the excess liquid to drain off.

3. Taking a spring roll wrapper, place it so that it is in a diamond position. Place a good handful of the filling into the bottom third of the wrapper. Draw the bottom point over the filling, and holding onto the top third of the pastry, draw the pastry covering the filling towards you, forming a tight package.

4. Roll over once. Then fold in the sides and continue to roll tightly into a cigar shape. Seal the spring roll with some water and flour paste.

5. Deep-fry at 170–180°C for 4 minutes or until pale golden. Serve with Worcester sauce and tomato sauce mixed together in equal quantities.

Measurements	Ingredients
2 tbsp	Oil
6 oz	Bean sprouts
2 oz	Carrots (shredded)
1 oz	Bamboo shoots (shredded)
1 tbsp	Wood ear (shredded and soaked)
1 oz	Cooked chicken (chopped or shredded)
1 oz	Ham or barbecued pork (shredded)
1 oz	Shrimps (cooked)
$\frac{1}{2}$ tsp	Salt
$\frac{1}{4}$ tsp	Sugar
Dash	White pepper and sesame oil
7–8	Spring roll wrappers
	Thick water/flour paste for sealing
	Oil for deep-frying

Beancurd Puffs

Variation of Pi Pa Beancurd

Method

1. Place the sieved beancurd into a bowl. Add all the other ingredients and mix well.

Measurements	Ingredients
8 oz	Beancurd (sieved and drained)
3 oz	Marinated chicken (chopped)

continued over →

2. Heat the oil in a wok to 170–180°C. Using a Chinese soup spoon (1 inch diameter), spoon turtle-egg-sized portions of the bean curd mix and gently drop into the hot oil. Deep-fry for 3–4 minutes until golden and cooked through. Drain onto kitchen paper. Repeat until all the mixture is used up.

3. Prepare the sauce. Heat the oil in a wok, add the chives and cook for 30 seconds. Add the ham and the mushrooms. Cook for a further 30 seconds. Add the wine and cook off. Add the stock and bring to the boil. Add the oyster sauce and the soy sauces.

4. Taste and correct the seasoning. Thicken with potato starch. Add a dash of white pepper and sesame oil. Turn down the heat and add the chopped spring onion. Pour over the beancurd puffs. Serve hot.

...continued

Measurements	Ingredients
4–6	Tinned Chinese mushrooms (diced)
1	Spring onion (chopped)
1 tbsp	Coriander (chopped)
1½ tbsp	Potato starch
1 level tsp	Salt
½ tsp	Sugar
Large pinch	White pepper
Dash	Sesame oil
1	Egg yolk
Sauce	Ingredients
1 tbsp	Oil
2 oz	Chinese chives (cut into 1 inch lengths)
2 oz	Sliced ham (shredded)
8–10	Chinese mushrooms (shredded)
1 tbsp	Shao Xing wine
6 fl oz	Stock
1 tbsp	Oyster sauce
2 tsp	Light soy sauce
1 tsp	Dark soy sauce
	Salt and sugar to taste
	Potato starch and water for thickening
Pinch	White pepper
Dash	Sesame oil

Lemon Chicken

Measurements	Ingredients
2 (approx. 12–16 oz)	Chicken breasts
$\frac{1}{2}$ tsp	Salt
Pinch	Sugar
Pinch	Ground white pepper
Dash	Sesame oil
$\frac{1}{2} - \frac{3}{4}$ tsp	Potato starch
	Oil for deep-frying
Batter	**Ingredients**
2 oz	Self-raising flour
1 oz	Potato starch
Pinch	Salt
1	Egg
5 fl oz	Cold water
1 tbsp	Oil
Lemon Sauce	**Ingredients**
5 oz	White/rice vinegar
5 oz	Sugar
5 fl oz	Water
1	Lemon (minced)
	Salt to taste
	Potato starch to thicken

Method

1. Split the chicken breasts into two pieces. Add the salt, sugar, white pepper and sesame oil and leave to marinate for 30–60 minutes.

2. To make the batter mix the flour, potato starch and salt in a bowl. Add the egg and cold water and mix until it has formed a thick batter. Leave for 15–20 minutes then add the oil.

3. To make the lemon sauce, combine all the ingredients except the potato starch in a wok and simmer for 15 minutes. Taste and correct the seasoning, thicken with a little potato starch if necessary, and pass through a sieve. Place to one side.

4. Heat a wok half full of oil to 190°C. Dip the chicken breasts into the potato starch, shake off the excess and dip into the batter. Carefully lower the battered chicken into the oil and fry for 5–6 minutes until the chicken is cooked and the batter is light golden and crispy. Remove and drain.

5. Cut the chicken into 2cm thick batons and assemble on a plate garnished with lemon slices. Pour the sauce around the chicken (not over it) to form a small pool. Serve hot.

Sesame Chicken

Method

1. Slice the chicken breast at an angle to get flat, thin slices.

2. Add the salt, pepper, sugar, potato starch and wine to the chicken breasts and mix thoroughly.

3. Add the egg yolk and mix. If necessary (if it is too runny), add more potato starch to get a thick paste-like covering. Add a dash of sesame oil.

4. Place the white untoasted sesame seeds on a tray, and press each slice of chicken breast onto the seeds, ensuring good adhesion and covering. Repeat until all the pieces of chicken breast are done.

5. Heat a wok half full of oil to 180°C. Carefully add one-third of the coated chicken pieces and fry for 3–4 minutes until the chicken is cooked and the sesame seeds are golden. Repeat with the remaining chicken, and drain on kitchen paper.

6. Serve hot with lemon wedges and Worcester sauce.

Measurements	Ingredients
1 (6–8oz)	Chicken breast
$\frac{1}{2}$ tsp	Salt
$\frac{1}{4}$ tsp	Sugar
2 tsp	Potato starch
1 tsp	Shao Xing wine
1	Egg yolk
Dash	White pepper
Dash	Sesame oil
	White untoasted sesame seeds

Chef's Notes

- Do not let the chicken pieces rest on the bottom of the wok as the sesame seeds are liable to burn. Gentle stirring with a spatula will prevent this.

Deep-fried Shredded Beef in Spicy Sauce

Measurements	Ingredients
8 oz	Topside of beef, cut into 3mm x 3mm x 60mm shreds, marinated (page 62)
1	Egg
	Potato starch for dredging
	Oil for deep-frying
2 tsp	Oil
3 oz	Carrot (shredded)
2	Spring onions (shredded)
$\frac{1}{2}$	Onion (shredded)
5 fl oz	Simply spicy sauce (page 66)
	Ground white pepper
	Sesame oil

Method

1. Mix the marinated shredded beef with the egg.

2. Dredge the beef shreds in the potato starch so that each one is well coated.

3. Heat a wok half full of oil, to 190°C, and deep-fry the beef in two batches, each for 2–3 minutes. Remove and drain on kitchen paper. Bring the oil back up to 190°C, and re-fry the beef until it no longer foams. Remove and drain. The beef should be dry and crisp.

4. In a wok quickly fry the shredded carrot, onion and spring onion in the oil. Add half a wok ladle of simply spicy sauce and bring to the boil. Add the beef shreds and quickly turn them to coat in the sauce. Add more sauce if necessary, just enough to coat each piece of beef evenly.

5. Add a dash of sesame oil and ground white pepper. Serve hot.

'Cherry' Chicken Winglets with Spiced Salt and Chilli

Measurements	Ingredients
6	Chicken wings
$\frac{3}{4}$ tsp	Salt
1 tsp	Sugar
1 tsp	Soy sauce
1 tsp	Rose liqueur
1 tbsp	Ginger (chopped)
$1\frac{1}{2}$ tsp	Potato starch
Pinch	Ground white pepper
Dash	Sesame oil
6oz	Prawn paste
2 tsp	Oil
$\frac{1}{2}$	Red chilli (sliced)
$\frac{1}{2}$	Green chilli (sliced)
Handful	Coriander leaves
2 tsp	Fried garlic flakes
$\frac{1}{2}$ tsp	Spiced salt (page 54)

Method

1. Cut the chicken wings into two pieces at the joint. Cut off the wing tip and set aside for stock. Cut through the tendons on the 'wing drumstick' and, using your fingers, push down around the joint to strip the meat from the bone. Then invert the flesh to form a pocket or the 'cherry'. Repeat this process with the wing portion, removing the thinner bone first.

2. Put the winglets into a bowl and add the salt, sugar, soy sauce, ginger, liqueur, potato starch, ground white pepper and sesame oil. Mix thoroughly, cover and leave to marinate for 3–4 hours or overnight if possible.

3. Using a dinner knife carefully stuff the prawn paste into the cavity of the winglets, taking care not to over-stuff, as the prawn paste will swell.

4. Coat the winglets in potato starch and deep-fry at 190°C for 5–6 minutes. Remove and drain.

5. In a wok, add the oil and bring to a high heat. Add the sliced chillies, coriander and chicken. Stir around, add the garlic flakes, season with a little spiced salt and serve with Worcester sauce and lemon wedges.

Quail with Spiced Salt, Chilli and Garlic

Method

1. Remove any remaining entrails and the windpipe from the quail. Rinse thoroughly to remove the blood and bits. Dry and set aside.

2. Mix the marinade in a bowl and then spoon into the cavity of the quail. Using a finger rub thoroughly inside. Rub the outside of the quail with a little salt.

3. Sit the quail upright in a colander and allow to marinate for 2 hours or overnight.

4. Dry off the quail and mop up any blood. Heat a wok half full of oil to around 170°C, and deep-fry the quail for around 5–6 minutes until golden. Remove and drain.

5. Split the quails into halves and place on a plate. In a hot wok with the oil add the chilli, garlic and spring onion. Fry until fragrant, then add the quail. Turn the quail in the spices, add a pinch of sugar and the spiced salt. Cook quickly for 30 seconds, then add some wine and the coriander.

6. Cook until the wine has gone and the coriander has wilted. Turn down the heat and add a dash of sesame oil.

7. Place the quails cut side down on a plate, then scrape over the fried bits. Garnish with a few fresh coriander leaves.

Measurements	Ingredients
1	Quail per person
1 tbsp	Oil
$\frac{1}{4}$ Red chilli	Sliced per quail
2 tsp	Garlic, fried per quail
$\frac{1}{2}$	Spring onion per quail
2 tbsp	Coriander leaves per quail
Pinch	Sugar
Pinch	Spiced salt (page 54)
Dash	Wine
	Sesame oil
Marinade	**Ingredients**
$\frac{1}{2}$ tsp	Salt per quail
$\frac{1}{4}$ tsp	Sugar per quail
$\frac{1}{8}$ tsp	Five-spice powder per quail
Pinch	Ground white pepper per quail

Mongolian Crispy Lamb

Method

1. If necessary, lightly flatten out the lamb. Rub the marinade on both sides of the lamb and leave to marinate overnight.

2. Place the lamb in a steam-proof dish with raised sides and steam for 45–60 minutes or until tender (it will break apart when pressed with a fork). Drain and leave to cool on a rack.

3. Heat a wok half to two-thirds full of oil to approx 190° C. Pat off any extra moisture on the lamb with a kitchen towel and deep-fry for 3–4 minutes until crispy. Remove and drain. The outside should be crispy and the inside still moist.

Measurements	Ingredients
$1\frac{1}{2}$ lb	Boneless lamb shoulder
	Oil for deep-frying
Marinade	Ingredients
1 tsp	Salt
2 tsp	Sugar
$\frac{1}{2}$ tsp	Five-spice powder
$\frac{1}{4}$ tsp	White pepper
2 tbsp	Rose liqueur
1 tbsp	Ginger (crushed and chopped)

4. To serve, shred the lamb with two forks and wrap in the pancakes with the cucumber, spring onion and a little sauce.

5. Serve with pancakes, cucumber batons, shredded spring onion and hoisin sauce.

Ribs with Chilli, Garlic and Spiced Salt

Method

1. Separate the ribs, then cut each one into pieces approximately 6 cm long. Rinse and pat dry.

2. Add all the marinade ingredients except the oil and work into the ribs. When they have absorbed as much of the potato starch as they can, add the oil and continue to work them until they become sticky. If it is too wet add a little potato starch to soak up the oil. Leave to marinate for 2–3 hours, or overnight.

3. Heat a wok half full of oil to 170°C. Coat the ribs in a little potato starch and deep-fry for 4–5 minutes until they are a golden brown. Drain and set aside.

4. Heat a clean wok until it is smoking. Add the oil then the chillies, peppercorns and the garlic. Cook until pungent. Add the ribs, spring onions, coriander, fried garlic flakes and sugar. Toss around until the sugar has melted and slightly caramelises.

5. Add the wine and toss the ribs until it has all evaporated. Turn down the heat and sprinkle evenly with the spiced salt and sesame oil.

Measurements	Ingredients
$1\frac{1}{2}$ lb	Baby back ribs
1 tbsp	Oil
1 small of each	Red and green chilli (sliced)
2 tsp	White peppercorns (crushed)
Large clove	Garlic (chopped)
1	Spring onion (chopped)
2 tbsp	Coriander leaves
1 tsp	Fried garlic flakes
Large pinch	Sugar
2 tbsp	Shao Xing wine
$\frac{1}{2}$ tsp	Spiced salt
Dash	Sesame oil
Marinade	Ingredients
$1\frac{1}{2}$ tsp	Salt
2 tsp	Sugar
$\frac{1}{4}$ tsp	Ground white pepper
$\frac{1}{8}$ tsp	Bicarbonate of soda
2 tbsp	Garlic (chopped)
2 tbsp	Ginger (chopped)
1 tbsp	Shao Xing wine
2 tbsp	Potato starch
2 tbsp	Oil

Sesame Prawn and Chicken Balls

Method

1. Mix the chicken, prawns, pork, coriander leaves, water chestnuts and marinade ingredients in a large bowl. Cover and leave to marinate for 2–3 hours or overnight.

2. Form the meat into 12 balls. Place in fridge to firm up for 20 minutes if necessary. Place on a plate and steam for 6–7 minutes. Allow to cool for 15 minutes.

3. Roll the balls in flour, followed by beaten egg, and finally in the sesame seeds.

4. Deep-fry in oil at 160°C for 4–5 minutes until golden.

5. Serve with chilli sauce, lemon wedges and Worcester sauce.

Measurements	Ingredients
6 oz	Chicken breast (chopped)
3 oz	Raw prawns (peeled, de-veined and roughly chopped)
3 oz	Fatty pork (minced)
1 tbsp	Coriander leaves (chopped)
1 tbsp	Water chestnuts (chopped)
100 g	Flour
1	Egg beaten
100 g	White sesame seeds
	Oil for deep-frying
Marinade	Ingredients
2 tsp	Potato starch
1 level tsp	Salt
1 tsp	Sugar
Large pinch	Bicarbonate of soda
Pinch	Pepper
2 tsp	Light soy sauce
2 tsp	Shao Xing wine
2 tbsp	Water

Salted Fish Rolls

Method

1. Place the slices of pork in a bowl and add all the marinade ingredients except the oil. Mix well, then finally add the oil and turn to coat the pieces. Cover and marinate for 30–60 minutes.

Measurements	Ingredients
6 thin slices (approx. 6 oz)	Pork loin
2 oz	Salted fish, dried or in oil, de-boned and cut into strips

continued over →

2. Place each of the pieces of pork between two layers of cling film and gently bat out to form a large thin circle, about 4–5 inches across. Spread a little sesame oil on the surface of the pork.

3. In the centre, place one-sixth of the strips of salted fish and one-sixth of the shredded ginger. Roll up like a spring roll, with the flap on the bottom. Place onto an oiled plate and repeat with the remaining ingredients.

4. Loosely cover with foil and steam for 5 minutes. Remove and drain on kitchen paper. Then roll each one into potato starch while still hot. Set aside.

5. Heat a wok one-third full of oil to around 180–190° C. Add the rolls and deep-fry for 1–2 minutes until golden. Remove and drain. Serve with Worcester sauce or sweet and sour sauce.

...continued

6 thin slices	Root ginger (finely shredded)
	Sesame oil
	Potato starch for dredging
	Oil for deep-frying
Marinade	Ingredients
$\frac{1}{2}$ tsp	Potato starch
$\frac{1}{2}$ tsp	Salt
$\frac{1}{2}$ tsp	Sugar
Pinch	White pepper
1 tsp	Shao Xing wine
1 tsp	Oil

Soft Shell Crabs with Chilli, Garlic and Spiced Salt

Method

1. Check under the carapace of the crab for any remaining gills, remove. Pull out the stomach sack from the face of the crab and discard.

2. Place the crab in the palm of one hand and then press with the other to remove any excess liquid. Place onto kitchen paper to drain further.

3. Roll crab in the beaten egg white and then firmly into the potato starch. Place onto a plate to allow the starch to fully adhere to the crab.

4. Deep-fry the crab at 190° C for 3–4 minutes until golden brown. Drain onto kitchen paper.

5. Add the oil to a hot wok then add the chillies, peppercorns, minced garlic, spring onions and coriander leaves.

Measurements	Ingredients
2 medium	Soft shell crabs per person
1	Egg white (beaten)
	Potato starch to coat
1 tbsp	Oil
To finish (per person)	Ingredients
$\frac{1}{2}$	Red chilli (sliced)
$\frac{1}{2}$	Green chilli (sliced)
$\frac{1}{2}$ tsp	White peppercorns (crushed)

continued over →

6. Cook until it becomes pungent, add the crabs and toss in the aromatics. Add a dash of Shao Xing wine and cook off. Season with the sugar and salt. Add the fried garlic flakes, turn to coat, add a dash of sesame oil and serve.

...continued

To finish (per person)	Ingredients
1 clove	Garlic (minced)
$\frac{1}{2}$	Spring onion (sliced)
1 large tbsp	Coriander leaves
Dash	Shao Xing wine
	Sugar and spiced salt (page 54) to taste
1 tsp	Fried garlic flakes
Dash	Sesame oil

Honey, Ginger and Lemon Chicken

Method

1. Mix the cubed chicken with the marinade ingredients, forming a sticky mass. Add more potato starch if required.

2. Leave to marinate for 2–3 hours or overnight if possible. Press the chicken into the potato starch and leave to absorb the moisture for 30 minutes.

3. Mix the sauce ingredients in a bowl. Deep-fry the chicken at 170° C for 2 minutes. Remove and drain.

4. Reheat the oil to 190° C and refry the chicken for 2 minutes more until pale golden in colour, not dark. Remove and drain.

5. Pour the sauce ingredients into a clean wok and bring to the boil. Taste and correct the seasoning. Add the chicken and the ginger shreds. Mix well to coat the chicken.

6. Serve on a plate garnished with lemon slices and chilli flowers.

Measurements	Ingredients
6–7 oz	Chicken breast (cubed)
	Potato starch for dredging
3 tbsp	Deep-fried ginger shreds for garnish
Marinade	Ingredients
$\frac{1}{2}$ tsp	Salt
1 tsp	Soy sauce
1 tsp	Sugar
Pinch	Ground white pepper
1	Egg yolk
2 tbsp	Potato starch
2 tsp	Oil
Honey Sauce	Ingredients
3 tbsp	Clear honey
2 tbsp	Lemon juice
3 tbsp	Water
$\frac{1}{2}$ tsp	Sugar
$\frac{1}{4}$ tsp	Salt
1 tbsp	Ginger juice

Aromatic Crispy Duck – Easy Version

Method

Measurements	Ingredients
1 (4½ lb)	Duck (split into 2, backbone removed)
5–6 tbsp	Chinese spice pot mix
1 inch	Ginger (crushed)
2 tsp	White peppercorns (crushed)
3 tbsp	Salt to taste
2 tbsp	Sugar to taste
	Oil for deep-frying

1. Place the duck into a deep pot that is also wide enough for it to lie down in.

2. Wrap the spices in some muslin and place in the pot with the duck. Add the ginger.

3. Cover with water, add the salt and sugar. Bring to the boil and then turn down the heat to a low simmer. Skim off the scum as it rises.

4. Taste the water and correct the seasoning so that it is slightly salty and sweet.

5. Simmer for 1–1½ hours until tender. Remove from the water and quickly remove the breast bones and the pelvic bones. Allow to cool on a rack, skin side up.

6. Once cool, place in the fridge and leave overnight to 'set'.

7. Heat oil in a wok to around 190°–200° C. Deep-fry the duck, skin side down first, for 3–4 minutes. Turn over and fry for a further 3–4 minutes, until the duck is golden and crispy.

8. Remove and drain on kitchen paper.

9. Place duck onto a plate and pull apart with two forks, removing the leg and wing bones as they appear.

10. Serve with pancakes, fresh cucumber batons, pickled cucumber batons, pickled carrot batons, shredded spring onion whites and hoisin sauce.

Aromatic Crispy Duck

Method

1. Rub the duck all over (and inside) with the Rose liqueur. Mix all the marinade ingredients together and rub the duck thoroughly, inside and out. Cover and leave to marinate overnight.

2. Place the duck onto a heatproof tray and steam for 2–3 hours until tender. Remove the breast and pelvic bones while hot. Remove to a rack (skin side up) and allow to cool. Place in the fridge overnight.

3. Heat oil in a wok to 190–200° C and deep-fry the duck for 3–4 minutes. Turn over and fry for a further 3–4 minutes until golden and crispy. Remove and drain on kitchen paper.

4. Place onto a plate and shred with 2 forks, removing the wing and leg bones as they appear.

5. Serve with pancakes, fresh and pickled cucumber batons, pickled carrot batons, shredded spring onion whites and hoisin sauce.

Chef's Notes

- Five-spice powder can also be used as a marinade.

Measurements	Ingredients
1 ($4\frac{1}{2}$–$5\frac{1}{2}$ lb)	Duck (whole or split in 2, backbone removed)
2–3 tbsp	Rose liqueur
4 tbsp	Salt
2 tbsp	Sugar
$\frac{1}{2}$ tsp	Ground white pepper
2	Spring onions (crushed)
1 inch	Ginger (crushed)
	Oil for deep-frying
Marinade	Ingredients
3	Star anise (crushed)
1	Grass fruit (crushed)
$1\frac{1}{2}$ tbsp	Cassia bark (crushed)
1 tbsp	Sichuan peppercorns (crushed and roasted)
2 tsp	White peppercorns (crushed)

Stir-fried Dishes

13

Squid with Chilli and Shrimp Paste

Measurements	Ingredients
8 oz	Prepared squid
1 tbsp	Oil
6–8 large	Spring onions cut into 1 inch pieces
1	Red chilli (sliced and deseeded)
1 tsp	Shrimp paste
1 tsp	Sugar
1 tbsp	Shao Xing wine
2 tbsp	Stock
Dash	Sesame oil
Pinch	White pepper

Method

1. Bring a wok of water to boil. Place the prepared squid into a spider and dip into the boiling water briefly, so that the squid just curls up, but is still raw inside. Drain and set aside.

2. In a wok, heat the oil to a medium heat. Add the spring onions and chilli and cook until fuming (you will know when this happens!). Add the squid, shrimp paste and sugar and quickly stir for 15 seconds. Add the wine and cook off the alcohol. Add the stock and cook for a further 30–45 seconds.

3. Taste and correct the seasoning. Turn down the heat, add the sesame oil and white pepper, and serve.

Chef's Notes

- There should be very little liquid left due to the high heat at which this dish is cooked, so no thickening is required.

Stir-fried Fillet of Fish with Asparagus

Method

1. Slice the fish into $\frac{1}{2}$ inch × 2 inch strips and marinate with the potato starch, salt, sugar, pepper and half the oil. Leave for 30 minutes.

2. Trim the asparagus and slice on the diagonal. Blanch for 1 minute along with the carrot and straw mushrooms. Drain and keep warm.

3. Mix the sauce ingredients together, except for the potato starch, and set aside.

4. Heat the remaining oil in a wok and add the ginger shreds. Stir around for a moment, then add the fish. Stir around until the fish becomes opaque, add the wine and the carrots and mushrooms and the garlic flakes. Cook over a high heat and slowly add the sauce, never allowing the heat to drop.

5. Taste, correct the seasoning and thicken if necessary. Scoop out onto a plate and serve hot.

Measurements	Ingredients
8 oz	Firm white fish fillet (halibut, turbot, Dover sole)
1 tsp	Potato starch
$\frac{1}{2}$ tsp	Salt
$\frac{1}{4}$ tsp	Sugar
Pinch	White pepper
2 tbsp	Oil
12 oz	Asparagus
10–12	Carrot (slices)
10–12	Straw mushrooms
3 slices	Ginger (shredded)
1 tbsp	Shao Xing wine
1 tsp	Fried garlic flakes
Sauce	Ingredients
2 fl oz	Chicken stock
$1\frac{1}{2}$ tsp	Oyster sauce
	White pepper
	Sesame oil
	Potato starch/water

Squid with Green Peppers and Black Bean Sauce

Method

1. Bring a wok to a high heat, add 2 tablespoons oil and add the onions, peppers, garlic and spring onions. Stir-fry for about 1 minute. Add the squid and black bean sauce and stir quickly for 30 seconds. Add the wine and cook off the alcohol. Add the stock, sugar and soy sauces and cook for a further minute.

2. Taste and correct the seasoning. Thicken if required. Turn down the heat, add a dash of sesame oil and white pepper and serve hot.

Measurements	Ingredients
2 tbsp	Oil
$\frac{1}{2}$	Onion (cut into $\frac{3}{4}$ inch squares)
2	Green peppers (deseeded and cut into $\frac{3}{4}$ inch diamonds)
1 clove	Garlic (roughly chopped)
2	Spring onions (cut into $\frac{3}{4}$ inch pieces)
12 oz	Prepared squid
1 tbsp	Black bean sauce for stir-frying
1 tbsp	Shao Xing wine
5 tbsp	Stock
$\frac{1}{2}$ tsp	Sugar
$\frac{1}{2}$ tsp	Dark soy sauce
1 tsp	Light soy sauce
Dash	Sesame oil
Dash	White pepper
	Potato starch/water for thickening

Clams/Mussels with Black Bean Sauce

Method

1. If using mussels, scrape off the barnacles and de-beard. Steam for 5 minutes until just open. Discard any that are still closed. Remove half the shell, leaving the mussel meat on the half shell. Remove the remaining beard. Reserve the steaming juices and add stock to make up to half a wok ladle.

Measurements	Ingredients
2 tbsp	Oil
1	Red chilli (deseeded and sliced)

continued over →

...continued

2. Heat a wok to a high heat. Add the oil and then the chilli, garlic, spring onions and the clams/mussels. Toss the shellfish for around a minute then add the wine and black bean sauce and cook for a further minute.

3. Add the stock and cover. Steam the shellfish for 2 minutes. Remove the lid and toss the shellfish around to absorb the flavours. Add the dark soy sauce, taste and correct the seasoning. Thicken if necessary.

Measurements	Ingredients
2 cloves	Garlic (chopped)
3	Spring onions (cut into 2 cm pieces)
2lb	Live farmed mussels or purged clams
1 tbsp	Shao Xing wine
1½ tbsp	Black bean sauce for stir-frying
½ wok ladle	Stock
1 tsp	Dark soy sauce
Dash	Sesame oil
Dash	White pepper
	Potato starch/ water for thickening

Oysters with Ginger and Spring Onions

Method

1. Bring a wok of water to the boil, add the oysters and gently poach for 30 seconds. Remove and drain. The oysters should still be raw on the inside.

2. Heat the oil in a wok to a medium heat. Add the ginger and the spring onion and turn for 1 minute. Add the oysters and the garlic flakes and continue to cook for 1 minute.

3. Add the wine and cook off the alcohol. Add the stock, oyster sauce, soy sauce, and sugar and cook over a high heat for 30 seconds. Thicken if necessary. Turn down the heat and add the sesame oil and the white pepper. Turn out onto a serving dish and serve hot.

Chef's Notes

• Be gentle with the oysters when you are stir-frying otherwise they will break up into a mush.

Measurements	Ingredients
10 oz	Oyster meat
1 tbsp	Oil
5 slices	Ginger (shredded)
1 bunch	Spring onions (cut into 3 cm pieces)
1 tsp	Fried garlic flakes
1 tbsp	Shao Xing wine
2 tbsp	Stock
2 tsp	Oyster sauce
1 tsp	Light soy sauce
½ tsp	Sugar
Dash	Sesame oil
Pinch	White pepper
	Potato starch/water for thickening

Beef with Peppers in Black Bean Sauce

Method

1. Deseed peppers and cut into 1 inch squares. Peel onion and cut into squares. Set aside.

2. Bring a wok one-quarter full of oil to a high heat. Run the beef through the oil and drain. Set aside. Clean wok if necessary.

3. Heat the wok to a high heat and add the oil. Add the onion, peppers and the garlic. Cook for 1 minute then add the beef and the black bean sauce. Stir around for another minute then add some wine and the stock.

4. Cook for a further 30 seconds then add dark soy sauce for colour and the oyster sauce. Stir and taste. Correct the seasoning and thicken with potato starch if necessary.

5. Turn down the heat and add some sesame oil. Serve hot.

Measurements	Ingredients
1	Green pepper
1	Red pepper
1	Onion
8 oz	Beef (marinated)
1 tbsp	Oil
1 clove	Garlic (chopped)
1 tbsp	Black bean sauce
2 tbsp	Shao Xing wine
$\frac{1}{2}$ ladle	Stock
	Dark soy sauce
1 tbsp	Oyster sauce
	Salt and pepper
	Sesame oil
	Oil for frying

Chef's Notes

• This can be served on top of crunchy noodles. To do this, add three-quarters of a ladle of stock after the wine has cooked off and proceed as above.

Chicken with Cashew Nuts

Method

1. Heat a wok one-third full of oil to a high heat and run the chicken breast cubes through the oil for 1 minute. Remove and drain.

Measurements	Ingredients
6 oz	Chicken breast cubes, marinated (see page 61)
2 tbsp	Oil
1	Carrot (cut into $\frac{1}{2}$ inch cubes and blanched)
1 medium	Bamboo shoot cut into $\frac{1}{2}$ inch cubes and blanched
8	Water chestnuts (quartered)

continued over →

...continued

2. Heat 2 tablespoons oil in a wok to a medium heat and add the carrot, bamboo shoots, water chestnuts and garlic. Stir-fry for 30 seconds and then add the chicken. Stir around then add the stock and cook until 1–2 tablespoons remain.

3. Add the sauces and the wine and cook until coated all around the chicken. Taste and correct the seasoning.

4. Add the spring onion and sesame oil and stir in. Scoop onto a plate and sprinkle with the cashew nuts.

Measurements	Ingredients
1 clove	Garlic (chopped)
$\frac{1}{4}$ ladle	Stock
2 tsp	Hoisin sauce combined with
2 tsp	Yellow bean sauce
Dash	Shao Xing wine
1	Spring onion (chopped)
	Sesame oil
3 tbsp	Prepared cashew nuts (see page 53)
	Oil for frying

Chicken/Beef with Mixed Vegetables

Method

1. Heat a wok one-third full of oil to a high heat. Run the meat through the oil for about 30–40 seconds. Remove and drain.

2. Heat the oil in a wok to a high heat and add the vegetables and garlic. Stir around for 1 minute.

3. Add the meat and the wine. Stir for 30 seconds. Add the stock and the oyster sauce and cook for 2 more minutes. Taste and correct the seasoning. Thicken with potato starch if necessary. Add a dash of sesame oil. Scoop out onto a plate and serve hot with rice.

Measurements	Ingredients
6 oz	Chicken/beef (marinated)
2 tbsp	Oil
2 oz	Bamboo slices (blanched)
3 sliced	Water chestnuts
6–8 slices	Carrot
1 handful	Bean sprouts
5–6	Straw mushrooms
1 clove	Garlic (chopped)
2 tbsp	Shao Xing wine
3 fl oz	Stock
1 tbsp	Oyster sauce
Pinch	Salt and sugar
Dash	Sesame oil and white pepper
	Potato starch and water for thickening
	Oil for frying

Prawns with Asparagus

Measurements	Ingredients
1 bunch	Asparagus
12 medium	Prawns (marinated)
1 clove	Garlic (chopped)
1 tbsp	Oil
$\frac{1}{4}$ ladle	Stock
1 tbsp	Oyster sauce
1 tbsp	Shao Xing wine
	Salt and pepper to taste
	Potato starch and water for thickening
Dash	Sesame oil
	Oil for frying

Method

1. Slice the asparagus on the diagonal. Heat a wok one-third full of oil to a high heat. Run the prawns through the oil for 15–20 seconds. Remove and drain.

2. Gently fry the garlic in the oil. Add the asparagus and cook for 1 minute. Add the stock and the oyster sauce and bring to the boil. Cook for a further minute. Add the prawns and wine, taste and correct the seasoning. Thicken if necessary. Add a dash of sesame oil.

3. Scoop out onto a plate and serve hot.

Crab 'Baked' with Ginger and Spring Onions

Measurements	Ingredients
1 (approx. $1\frac{1}{2}$–2 lb)	Live crab
2 tbsp	Oil
1 inch	Ginger (crushed and roughly chopped)
6 cloves	Garlic (crushed and roughly chopped)
2 bunches	Spring onions (greens and whites separated)
1 tbsp	Brandy
$1\frac{1}{2}$ tsp	Sugar
4–6 fl oz	Stock
	Dark soy sauce
1 tbsp	Light soy sauce
1–2 tbsp	Oyster sauce
	Potato starch/water for thickening
Dash	Sesame oil
	Oil for frying

Method

1. Chop up the crab (as per page 11). Set aside.

2. Heat a wok one-third full of oil to a high heat, and run the crab through the oil for 20–30 seconds. Remove and drain.

3. In a clean wok, add the oil and gently fry the ginger until fragrant and beginning to brown. Add the garlic and the spring onion whites and continue to cook until soft and translucent.

4. Bring the wok containing the ginger, garlic and spring onion whites to a high heat and add the crab. Add the brandy and sugar and cook off the alcohol. Add the stock, soy sauces and oyster sauce and cover. Cook for 1 minute covered, then remove the lid and continue to cook with stirring for 2–3 minutes.

5. Add the spring onion greens and thicken with the potato starch if required. Turn down the heat, add a dash of sesame oil and serve hot.

Chef's Notes

- This dish can be served on top of crunchy noodles.

Crab Baked with Black Bean Sauce

Method

1. Chop up the live crab (see page 11 for instructions).

2. Heat a wok one-third full of oil to a high heat and run the pieces of crab through the oil for 20–30 seconds.

3. In a clean wok, heat the oil and add the shredded onion. Cook over a high heat for 30 seconds, then add the ginger, garlic and red chilli. Cook until pungent. Add the prepared black bean sauce and the crab. Stir around for 10 seconds then add the brandy and the stock.

4. Cover and cook for 1 minute, then remove the lid and cook for 2–3 minutes. Add the dark soy to adjust the colour, followed by the light soy and the sugar.

5. Taste and correct the seasoning. Thicken if required. Turn down the heat, add a dash of sesame oil and some ground white pepper, mix and serve hot.

Measurements	Ingredients
1 (approx. 1½–2 lb)	Live crab
2 tbsp	Oil
1 medium	Onion (shredded)
½ tbsp each	Garlic and ginger (chopped)
1	Red chilli (deseeded and shredded)
1 tbsp	Black bean sauce
1 heaped tbsp	Brandy
4–6 fl oz	Stock
Dash	Dark soy sauce
1 tbsp	Light soy sauce
2 tsp	Sugar
	Potato starch/water for thickening
	Sesame oil
	Ground white pepper
	Oil for frying

Chef's Notes

• This dish can be served on a bed of crunchy noodles.

Sichuan Beans

Measurements	Ingredients
10 oz	French beans
2 tbsp	Oil
2 tbsp	Dried shrimps (coarsely chopped)
3 cloves	Garlic (chopped)
$\frac{1}{2}$	Red chilli (chopped)
$\frac{1}{2}$ tsp	Sugar
2 tbsp 1 tbsp	Hot bean sauce *or* Chilli oil
2 tbsp	Shao Xing wine
1 tbsp	Light soy sauce
2 tbsp	Red vinegar
2 tbsp	Chinkiang vinegar
	White pepper
Dash	Sesame oil
	Oil for frying

Method

1. Top and tail the beans. Wash and dry. Heat a wok one-third full of oil to a high heat and deep-fry the beans for 1 minute until slightly brown and wrinkly. Remove and drain.

2. Heat the oil in a wok to a medium heat. Add the shrimps and the garlic and cook until beginning to brown. Add the chilli, and when pungent, add the beans and the sugar.

3. Cook for 30 seconds, then add the chilli sauce or oil and the wine. Cook with the lid off until the wine has evaporated. Turn off the heat, add the soy sauce, vinegar, pepper and sesame oil. Mix well and serve hot.

Spinach with Garlic

Method

1. Blanch the spinach leaves in boiling salted water for 20 seconds until wilted. Drain in a colander.

2. Heat the oil in a wok and add the garlic. Fry quickly until beginning to brown, then add the spinach, salt and sugar. Quickly stir-fry for 30 seconds and then add the wine. Cook until the wine has evaporated.

3. Taste and correct the seasoning. Add a dash of sesame oil and serve hot.

Measurements	Ingredients
1lb	Spinach (washed and drained)
3 tbsp	Oil
4 large cloves	Garlic (chopped)
$\frac{1}{2}$ tsp	Salt
$\frac{1}{2}$ tsp	Sugar
2 tbsp	Shao Xing wine
Dash	White pepper
	Sesame oil

Spinach with Fermented Shrimp Paste

Method

1. Blanch the spinach in boiling salted water until just wilted. Drain in a colander.

2. Heat the oil in a wok and add the garlic and the chilli. Quickly fry until just beginning to brown, then add the shrimp paste and stir into the oil. Add the spinach and stir around for 20 seconds. Add the sugar and the wine and cook until the wine has evaporated.

3. Taste and correct the seasoning. Thicken with a little potato starch, add a dash of sesame oil. Serve hot.

Measurements	Ingredients
1lb	Spinach (washed and drained)
3 tbsp	Oil
2 large cloves	Garlic (chopped)
$\frac{1}{2}$	Red chilli (chopped)
1 tsp	Fermented shrimp paste
2 tsp	Sugar
2 tbsp	Shao Xing wine
Pinch	Salt
Dash	White pepper
	Potato starch and water
	Sesame oil

Duck with Two Bean Sauces

Method

1. Place the coriander leaves onto a large serving plate.

2. Combine all the sauces, the sugar and 1 tablespoon of the wine in a bowl.

3. Bring a wok to a high heat and add the oil. Add the duck and cook until 70% done. Add the bowl of sauce and stir vigorously. Add more wine if necessary to prevent sticking.

4. Cook the duck on a high heat until done and the sauce just coats all the pieces, with none left in the wok. Turn off the heat and add a dash of sesame oil and white pepper. Pile on top of the coriander and serve hot.

Measurements	Ingredients
Large bunch	Coriander leaves (washed and dried)
1 tbsp	Yellow bean sauce
2 tbsp	Hoisin sauce
1 tsp	Dark soy sauce
1 tsp	Oyster sauce
1 tsp	Soy sauce
1 tsp	Sugar
4 tbsp	Shao Xing wine
2 tbsp	Oil
8 oz	Marinated duck breast, sliced (see page 63)
Dash	Sesame oil
	White pepper

Chicken with Pineapple

Method

1. Mix the chicken strips with the marinade ingredients, adding the oils last of all. Leave to marinate for 1½–2 hours.

2. Heat the wok, add half the oil and swirl around. Add the ginger shreds and fry briefly for 1 minute. Add the chicken breast and cook over a high heat for 2 minutes or until the chicken becomes opaque. Remove to serving dish and keep warm

3. Clean the wok, add the remaining oil and bring to a high heat. Add the onions, pepper and carrot and cook for 1 minute. Add the chicken and cook for a further 3 minutes. Add just enough sweet and sour sauce to coat the chicken and vegetables.

4. Add the pineapple, a dash of white pepper and sesame oil and turn over a few times to warm the pineapple. Serve hot.

Measurements	Ingredients
12 oz	Chicken breast (cut into strips)
2 tbsp	Oil
3 slices	Ginger (cut into shreds)
½ large	Onion (cut into ¾ inch squares)
1	Green pepper (deseeded and cut into ¾ inch squares)
12–16 slices	Carrot
4 fl oz	Sweet and sour sauce
3	Pineapple rings (tinned, cut into 18 pieces)
	Sesame oil

Marinade	Ingredients
⅔ tsp	Salt
¼ tsp	Sugar
1 tsp	Light soy sauce
1 tsp	Potato starch
1 tsp	Vegetable oil
Dash	Sesame oil
Dash	White pepper
Dash	Shao Xing wine

Duck with Pineapple and Pickled Ginger

Measurements	Ingredients
3 oz	Pineapple rings (tinned)
2 oz	Pickled ginger (sliced)
2 tsp	Oil
8 oz	Marinated duck breast (see page 63)
1 clove	Garlic (crushed)
$\frac{1}{4}$	Green pepper (shredded)
4 tbsp	Chicken stock
1 tbsp	Oyster sauce
	Dark soy sauce for colour adjustment
	Potato starch for thickening
Dash	White pepper and sesame oil

Method

1. Cut the pineapple rings into 18 pieces. Cut the pickled ginger into smaller slices if too large.

2. Heat the oil in a wok, add the duck, stir-fry for 1 minute, then add the garlic and green pepper and continue to cook for a further 2 minutes. Add the pineapple, pickled ginger and a touch of stock if it looks too dry. Add the oyster sauce and a little dark soy sauce to deepen the colour, and continue to cook for 1 more minute.

3. Taste, correct the seasoning, and thicken with potato starch if necessary. Add a dash of white pepper and sesame oil, place onto a serving dish and serve hot.

Chef's Notes

- Tinned pineapple needs minimal cooking, just enough heat to warm it through, or it will become sour beyond belief.

- Fresh pineapple can also be used, but use a very ripe and sweet one (Del Monte gold is recommended).

Duck with Mixed Vegetables

Method

1. Stir-fry or blanch the vegetables for 1 minute and set aside.

2. Heat the oil in a wok to a high heat and carefully add the prepared duck breast. Cook for 2 minutes then add the garlic. Add a splash of Shao Xing wine and cook off the alcohol.

3. Add the vegetables and cook for 1 minute. Add half the stock, the oyster sauce and a dash of white pepper. Cook for 1 more minute adding more stock if necessary.

4. Taste, correct the seasoning and thicken if required. Add a dash of sesame oil and serve hot.

Measurements	Ingredients
12 oz	Mixed vegetables (baby sweet corn, straw mushrooms, etc.)
2 tbsp	Oil
8 oz	Marinated duck breast, sliced/shredded
1 clove	Garlic (crushed)
Dash	Shao Xing wine
4–5 tbsp	Stock
1 tbsp	Oyster sauce
Dash	White pepper
Dash	Sesame oil

Duck with Coriander and Mixed Bean Sauce

Measurements	Ingredients
Large bunch	Coriander
2 tsp	Hoisin sauce
2 tsp	Crushed yellow bean sauce
$\frac{1}{2}$ tsp	Sugar
1 tbsp	Oil
8 oz	Marinated duck breast (shredded and prepared)
2 tbsp	Stock
Dash	Sesame oil
	White pepper

Method

1. Wash the coriander and pick over to remove any yellow or dead leaves. Then cut into 2 inch sections.

2. Combine the two sauces, add sugar to adjust the taste; it should be savoury sweet and not too salty.

3. Heat the wok to a high heat, add the oil and swirl around. Add the duck breast and cook for 2 minutes. Add the coriander, mixed bean sauce and stock and cook for 2 more minutes. Taste, correct the seasoning and thicken if necessary.

4. Add a dash of white pepper and sesame oil. Place on a dish and serve hot.

Beef with Mango

Measurements	Ingredients
½ medium	Mango
2 ladles	Oil
6 oz	Beef topside or fillet (marinated)
2 tbsp	Oil
3 thin slices	Ginger (shredded)
1	Spring onion (cut into slices)
	Sesame oil
Sauce	Ingredients
1 tbsp	Oyster sauce
1 tbsp	Shao Xing wine
½ tsp	Dark soy sauce
4 tbsp	Water
Pinch	Sugar
Pinch	Pepper

Method

1. Peel the mango with a fruit peeler and cut the flesh off in strips.

2. Mix all the ingredients for the sauce in a bowl.

3. In a hot wok add the oil and quickly run the beef through it. Drain the beef in a colander and set aside. Clean the wok.

4. Heat the remaining oil in the wok until smoking then add the shredded ginger and quickly stir. Add the beef and cook for 1 minute. Add all the sauce and cook until half remains.

5. Taste and correct the seasoning, add the mango and cook for about 30 seconds until hot.

6. Turn down the heat and add the spring onion and a little sesame oil. Turn and place onto plate. Garnish with chilli flowers.

Chicken with Peppers and Black Bean Sauce

Method

1. Place the chicken strips into a bowl and add the marinade ingredients except the oils. Mix thoroughly, then add the oils and turn the chicken to coat. Cover and leave to marinate for 2–3 hours.

2. Deseed the peppers and cut into $\frac{3}{4}$ inch squares. Do the same with the onion.

3. In a wok, heat the oil until smoking and add the chicken. Stir to separate the pieces. Cook for 1 minute, then add the onions and peppers and cook for another minute. Add a good slug of wine. Cook until gone.

4. Add the black bean sauce and cook for an additional minute. Add some stock if it seems a bit too thick.

5. Turn down the heat and add a dash of sesame oil to finish. Spoon onto serving dish and serve hot with rice.

Measurements	Ingredients
6–7 oz	Chicken breast (cut into strips)
$\frac{1}{2}$ each	Red, green and yellow peppers
$\frac{1}{4}$	Onion
1 tbsp	Oil
A little	Shao Xing wine
1 tbsp	Black bean sauce
A little	Stock
Dash	Sesame oil
Marinade	Ingredients
$\frac{1}{2}$ tsp	Potato starch
$\frac{1}{4}$ tsp	Salt
$\frac{1}{4}$ tsp	Sugar
Pinch	Pepper
Dash	Shao Xing wine
2 tsp	Water
2 tsp	Oil
Dash	Sesame oil

Lamb with Sweet Bean Sauce

Method

1. Mix the lamb with the marinade and leave for 2–3 hours or overnight.

2. In a hot wok, add half the oil and stir-fry the shredded leek whites for 1 minute with a pinch of salt and sugar. Place onto a serving plate in a little mound.

Measurements	Ingredients
6 oz	Leg of lamb or neck fillet (sliced)
2 tbsp	Oil
6 oz	Leek white (washed and thickly shredded)
2 tbsp	Shao Xing wine
1 tsp	Yellow bean sauce

continued over →

...continued

3. In a hot clean wok, add the remaining oil and then the lamb. Stir to separate the pieces. Cook for 1 minute then add the wine and cook off. Add the bean sauce, hoisin sauce, dark soy sauce and sugar, and a touch of water if required. Cook until the sauce reduces to a light syrupy consistency. Turn off the heat and add a dash of sesame oil and white pepper.

4. Pour off any liquid that may have drained from the leeks and scoop the lamb on top of them. Serve hot.

Measurements	Ingredients
1 tbsp	Hoisin sauce
Dash	Dark soy sauce for colour
1 tsp	Sugar
Dash	Sesame oil and white pepper
Marinade	**Ingredients**
$\frac{1}{4}$ tsp	Potato starch
$\frac{1}{8}$ tsp	Salt
$\frac{1}{8}$ tsp	Sugar
Pinch	Bicarbonate of soda
Pinch	Pepper
1 tsp	Rose liqueur
Dash	Soy sauce
1 tbsp	Water
1 tsp	Oil

Gai Lan with Ginger and Brandy

Measurements	Ingredients
6 oz	Chinese gai lan
1 tsp	Sugar
2 tbsp	Oil
3 slices	Ginger (finely shredded)
Pinch	Salt
Pinch	Sugar
2 tsp	Brandy diluted with 3 tbsp water
	Soy sauce

Method

1. Wash the gai lan carefully and cut each piece into 3 or 4.

2. Bring a wok half full of water to the boil. Add the sugar and then the gai lan. As soon as the water begins to boil, remove the gai lan from the water and allow to drain in a colander.

3. Heat a clean wok until hot. Add the oil and then the ginger. Stir quickly then add the drained gai lan, a pinch of salt followed by a pinch of sugar. Stir around for 15–20 seconds then add the diluted brandy.

4. Cook on a high heat until the brandy evaporates and there is hardly a trace of liquid left (no more than 30–45 seconds). Turn off the heat and scoop the gai lan onto a plate. Drizzle over a little soy sauce. Serve hot.

Lettuce Wrap

Method

1. Mix the meat with the marinade, adding the oil last. Cover and leave to marinate for 1–2 hours.

2. Add the oil to a hot wok, then add the garlic followed by the meat. Stir-fry until the mince is separated and half cooked.

3. Add the vegetables and the oysters, cook for 1 minute then add the wine. Once the wine has all evaporated, add the stock, dark soy sauce, oyster sauce and the sugar.

4. Cook for 2–3 minutes, then taste and correct the seasoning. Lightly thicken with potato starch, then increase the heat and reduce to the required consistency.

5. Turn off the heat, add a dash of sesame oil and white pepper. Garnish with chopped spring onion whites.

Measurements	Ingredients
2 oz	Shoulder of pork (chopped)
6 oz	Chicken breast (chopped)
2 tbsp	Oil
1 clove	Garlic, minced
1 oz	Bamboo shoots (chopped)
1 oz	Water chestnuts (chopped)
1 oz	Soaked Chinese mushrooms (diced)
1 oz	Sichuan preserved vegetable (chopped)
1 oz	Soaked dried oysters (chopped)
1 tbsp	Shao Xing wine
6 fl oz	Stock
$\frac{1}{2}$ tsp	Dark soy sauce
1 tbsp	Oyster sauce
$\frac{1}{4}$ tsp	Sugar
	Salt to taste

continued over →

Chef's Notes

...continued

- This dish is served wrapped in lettuce leaves.

Dash	Potato starch and water to thicken
	Sesame oil and white pepper
	Iceberg lettuce leaves to serve with
Marinade	**Ingredients**
$\frac{1}{2}$ tsp	Potato starch
$\frac{1}{4}$ tsp	Salt
$\frac{1}{8}$ tsp	Sugar
Pinch	Pepper
1 tsp	Shao Xing wine
Pinch	Bicarbonate of soda
1 tbsp	Water
2 tsp	Oil

Beef with Tomatoes

Method

1. Mix the sauce in a bowl then set aside.

2. Add half the oil to a hot wok, then quickly stir-fry the beef until it is half done. Remove to a plate, clean the wok.

3. Add the remaining oil to a hot wok and add the onions. Cook for 30 seconds, then add the beef, cook for a further 30 seconds, then add the sauce.

4. Cook until the sauce is reduced by half then add the tomatoes, and stir in gently to warm through.

5. Turn off the heat then add the spring onions, squeeze in a little lemon juice and a dash of sesame oil and white pepper.

6. Scoop onto a plate and serve hot with plain rice.

Measurements	Ingredients
2 tbsp	Oil
6 oz	Topside of beef (marinated)
$\frac{1}{2}$ large	Onion (shredded)
2	Tomatoes (peeled, quartered and deseeded)
1	Spring onion (sliced diagonally)
Squeeze (1$\frac{1}{2}$ tsp)	Lemon juice
Dash	White pepper
Dash	Sesame oil
Sauce	**Ingredients**
2 tbsp	Tomato sauce
1 tbsp	Light soy sauce
1$\frac{1}{2}$ tsp	Dark soy sauce
2 tsp	Sugar
2 fl oz	Shao Xing wine

Kung Pao Chicken

Measurements	Ingredients
10 oz	Chicken breast (cut into small cubes)
6	Spring onions (green sections only)
3 tbsp	Oil
1 oz	Dried red chillies
1 tsp	Sichuan peppercorns
1 tsp	Ginger (minced)
2 oz	Garlic peanuts or plain roasted peanuts
Marinade	Ingredients
1 tsp	Potato starch
$\frac{1}{2}$ tsp	Salt
1 tbsp	Light soy sauce
1 tsp	Sugar
Pinch	Bicarbonate of soda
1 tbsp	Oil
Sauce	Ingredients
2 tbsp	Water/stock
2 tsp	Sugar
1 tbsp	Dark soy sauce
1 tbsp	Shao Xing wine
1 tbsp	Rice vinegar
1 tbsp	Light soy sauce
Dash	Sesame oil

Method

1. Mix the chicken with the marinade ingredients, cover and place in fridge for 1 hour.

2. Mix the sauce ingredients together in a bowl and set aside.

3. Cut the spring onion greens into 1 inch sections.

4. Heat a wok until smoking, add 2 tablespoons oil and the chicken breasts. Cook for 1 minute until opaque. Remove to a plate.

5. Clean wok, add the remaining oil then add the chillies and the Sichuan peppercorns. Gently cook until pungent. Turn up the heat and add the spring onion greens and the minced ginger. Cook for 30 seconds.

6. Add the chicken and turn in the aromatics to absorb the flavours. Add the sauce ingredients and reduce by half. Taste and correct the seasoning.

7. Mix in the peanuts, scoop onto a plate and serve hot.

Peking Ribs

Measurements	Ingredients
1 lb	Baby back rib singles (cut into 2 inch lengths, rinsed and dried)
2 tbsp	Oil
Dash	Sesame oil and white pepper
2 fl oz	Shao Xing wine
Marinade	Ingredients
$\frac{1}{2}$ tsp	Salt
1 tsp	Sugar
2 tsp	Light soy sauce
2 tsp	Rose liqueur
2 tsp	Potato starch
Pinch	Bicarbonate of soda
Pinch	White pepper
1 tbsp	Water
1 tbsp	Oil
Sauce	Ingredients
2 fl oz	Water
4 fl oz	Chinkiang vinegar
5 oz	Sugar
$1\frac{1}{2}$ oz	Tomato sauce
2 fl oz	Red vinegar
2 slices	Lemon, no seeds (minced)
	Salt to taste

Method

1. Place the ribs into a bowl, add the marinade ingredients and mix well. Cover and place in the fridge for 1 hour.

2. Place all the sauce ingredients into a wok and slowly heat, stirring all the time to dissolve the sugar.

3. Once the sugar has dissolved, bring to boil, then turn down the heat and simmer for 2 minutes. Strain into a clean bowl and set aside.

4. Heat a clean wok and add 2 tablespoons oil. Add the ribs and stir-fry over a medium heat for 4–5 minutes.

5. Add the Shao Xing wine and cover. Once the wine has evaporated, add the sauce and cook for a further 2–3 minutes until the sauce is reduced and sticky. Taste and correct the seasoning.

6. Add a dash of sesame oil and white pepper. Scoop onto a plate and garnish with coriander or parsley.

Lamb with Honey

Method

1. Slice the lamb into thin slices and mix with the marinade. Cover and leave to marinate for 2–3 hours or overnight.

2. Mix all the sauce ingredients in a bowl and set aside.

3. Run the lamb through hot oil and drain. Clean the wok.

4. Add the oil to a hot wok. Add the vegetables and cook for 1 minute, add the lamb and the Sichuan peppercorns, cook for a further minute.

5. Add the sauce and reduce by half. Taste and correct the seasoning. Thicken if required.

6. Mix in the peanuts, add a dash of sesame oil and white pepper.

Measurements	Ingredients
8 oz	Lamb neck fillet or leg
2 tbsp	Oil
$\frac{1}{2}$	Red pepper (cut into squares)
$\frac{1}{2}$	Green pepper (cut into squares)
$\frac{1}{2}$ medium	Onion (cut into squares)
$\frac{1}{4}$ tsp	Sichuan peppercorns (ground and roasted)
3 tbsp	Raw peanuts, prepared as cashew nuts (see page 53)
	Potato starch and water for thickening
	Sesame oil and white pepper
	Oil for frying
Marinade	**Ingredients**
$\frac{1}{2}$ tsp	Potato starch
$\frac{1}{4}$ tsp	Salt, sugar
$\frac{1}{2}$ tsp	Rose liqueur
Pinch	Bicarbonate of soda, white pepper
2 tbsp	Water
1 tbsp	Oil
Dash	Sesame oil
Sauce	**Ingredients**
$1\frac{1}{2}$ tbsp	Honey
1 tbsp	Soy sauce
Pinch	Salt
1 tbsp	Orange juice
1 tsp	Dark soy sauce
1 tbsp	Wine
1 tbsp	Water

Sizzling Mongolian Lamb

Method

1. Mix the lamb with the marinade and cover. Leave to marinate for 2–3 hours or overnight if possible.

2. To prepare the sauce fry the garlic in the oil, add the remaining sauce ingredients and cook until hot. Taste and correct the seasoning and consistency. Set aside. Keep warm.

3. Place the iron plate onto the heat and leave on low for 5–6 minutes until hot.

4. Add the oil to a hot wok and stir-fry the lamb until cooked, adding a little wine if it sticks. Add a dash of sesame oil and white pepper.

5. Carefully put the hot iron plate onto its wooden base. Place the onion, spring onions, chilli and coriander onto the hot iron plate.

6. Carefully put the cooked lamb on top of the vegetables.

7. Place the platter onto the table. Pour the sauce into a sauce boat and bring to the table.

8. In front of your guests, pour the sauce evenly over the lamb and vegetables. The resulting steam is hot enough to finish cooking the vegetables.

Measurements	Ingredients
8 oz	Lamb neck fillet or leg (sliced)
1 tbsp	Oil
Dash	Sesame oil
Dash	Ground white pepper
$\frac{1}{2}$	Onion (sliced)
1 bunch	Spring onions (washed, trimmed and cut into 2 inch batons)
1	Red chilli (sliced into rings)
4 tbsp	Coriander leaves
Marinade	**Ingredients**
$\frac{1}{2}$ tsp	Potato starch
$\frac{1}{4}$ tsp	Salt and sugar
$\frac{1}{2}$ tsp	Rose liqueur
1 tbsp	Water
1 tbsp	Oil
Dash	Sesame oil
Sauce	**Ingredients**
1 clove	Garlic (minced)
1 tbsp	Oil
2 tbsp	Sa-cha sauce (Chinese satay)
1 tsp	Sesame sauce
1 tbsp	Hot bean sauce
2 tsp	Yellow bean sauce
2 tsp	Sugar
4 fl oz	Chicken stock

Mushroom with Crab

Method

1. Steam or poach fresh shiitake in lightly seasoned stock for 2–3 minutes, or steam braised shiitake until hot. Drain.

2. Place the stock and fried garlic into a wok and gently heat until simmering, season the stock and add the wine. Simmer for 1 minute. Remove the garlic.

3. Thicken the stock to a light consistency, and add the crab and warm through. Taste and correct the seasoning.

4. Turn off the heat and gently dribble in the egg white while slowly stirring, to form thin egg flowers. Add a dash of sesame oil.

5. Place the mushrooms, cap upwards, onto a warm plate and border with the greens. Dress the sauce evenly over the mushrooms.

6. Garnish with crab coral in a little pile in the centre.

Chef's Notes

- Deep-fried cooked Chinese ham is an alternative to the coral.

- Do not thicken the sauce too much as the egg white will thicken the sauce further.

Measurements	Ingredients
12	Shiitake mushrooms, fresh or braised *or*
1 tin	Straw mushrooms *or*
10 oz	Mixed mushrooms
8 fl oz	Chicken or chicken and ham stock
1 clove	Garlic, crushed and lightly fried until golden, and drained
1 tsp	Shao Xing wine
	Potato starch and water for thickening
4–5 oz	White crab meat in large pieces
1	Egg white (beaten)
	Sesame oil
6 oz	Green leaf vegetables (blanched, to border plate and mushrooms)
	Salt and white pepper for seasoning
1 tbsp	Crab coral, cooked and chopped, for garnish if available

Crab with Asparagus

Method

1. Quickly blanch the asparagus in boiling lightly salted water (30 seconds) to which 1 tablespoon oil has been added. Drain and refresh.

Measurements	Ingredients
1 bunch	Asparagus (peeled and cut into equal lengths)

continued over →

2. In a wok, add the oil and the shredded ginger. Fry lightly without colouring the ginger. Drain off the oil and add the stock.

3. Bring to a gentle simmer, add the dark soy sauce, oyster sauce and season with salt and white pepper.

4. Thicken to a light consistency and add the asparagus and crab leg meat. Warm through, taking care not to break up the crab.

5. Turn off the heat and add dash of sesame oil.

6. To serve, place the asparagus onto a plate in two rows, one of tips and the other of stems, approximating a spear of asparagus. Place the crab leg meat neatly on top of the asparagus, and pour over the remaining sauce.

7. Garnish with a sprinkle of the deep-fried Chinese ham shreds.

...continued

Measurements	Ingredients
1 tbsp	Oil
3 slices	Ginger (shredded)
6 fl oz	Stock
2 drops	Dark soy sauce
1 tsp	Oyster sauce
	Salt and white pepper
6 oz	Whole crab leg meat
	Potato starch and water to thicken
Dash	Sesame oil
	Deep-fried shredded Chinese ham

Stir-fried 'Milk'

Measurements	Ingredients
6	Egg whites
	Milk or milk/single cream equal in volume to the egg whites
$\frac{1}{2}$ tsp	Potato starch
4 oz	White crab meat (flaked)
1 tsp	Sesame oil
3 tbsp	Oil
1 oz	Deep-fried rice vermicelli
2 tbsp	Pine nuts (roasted)
	Deep-fried shredded Chinese ham
	Salt and white pepper to taste

Method

1. In a bowl, add the egg whites, milk/cream, potato starch and crab and whisk lightly until homogenised. Season and taste.

2. Whisk in the sesame oil.

3. In a wok, add the oil and heat until just beginning to smoke. Add the egg white mixture and quickly 'push' to form light flakes. Do not allow the egg white to colour.

4. 'Push' this mixture until just set, remove from heat.

5. Place the deep-fried rice vermicelli onto the plate in a heap in the centre. Carefully place over the set egg white. Garnish with the pine nuts and deep-fried ham.

Chef's Notes

- If over-cooked, the egg mixture will begin to weep. To remedy this, have some stock mixed with potato starch ready. This can be added to form a thin sauce that will hide the overcooked egg white.

Braised Dishes

14

Braised Fish with Beancurd Puffs and Straw Mushrooms

Method

1. Mix the fish with the seasoning and set aside for 30 minutes.

2. Heat the oil for frying in a wok and deep-fry the fish for 2 minutes. Drain and set aside.

3. In a wok, gently fry the ginger and spring onion in the oil. Add the sauce ingredients and bring to the boil. Add the beancurd puffs and straw mushrooms and place the fish gently on top. Simmer for 10–15 minutes until the beancurd puffs have softened and the fish is cooked through.

4. Taste, correct seasoning and thicken if necessary. Add a dash of white pepper and sesame oil. Garnish with some coriander and serve hot.

Measurements	Ingredients
7 oz	Grass carp (tail or fillet)
1 tsp	Ginger (minced)
2 tsp	Spring onion (minced)
2 tbsp	Oil
6–8	Beancurd puffs
12–16	Straw mushrooms
	Ground white pepper
	Sesame oil
	Fresh coriander leaves for garnish
	Oil for deep-frying
Seasoning	**Ingredients**
$\frac{1}{2}$ tsp	Salt
$\frac{1}{4}$ tsp	Shao Xing wine
$1\frac{1}{2}$ tbsp	Potato starch
Sauce	**Ingredients**
2 tsp	Sugar
$\frac{1}{4}$ tsp	Salt
1 tsp	Dark soy sauce
1 tbsp	Shao Xing wine
1 pint	Chicken stock
2 tsp	Yellow bean sauce

Braised Eel with Garlic

Method

1. Gut the eel. Rub with flour to remove as much slime as possible, then dip in boiling water and scrape off the remaining slime.

2. Cut the eel into $\frac{1}{2}$ inch thick rounds and quickly blanch in salted boiling water to remove the blood and impurities. Drain and leave to cool.

3. In a clean wok boil the garlic cloves for 5 minutes. Drain and pat dry. Slice the roast belly pork and set aside.

4. Heat some oil in wok to 150° C and gently fry the garlic cloves until a light golden brown. Lightly coat the eel with the potato starch. Heat the oil to 190° C and deep-fry the eel until golden. Drain.

5. Scrape the pith from the peel and set aside. In a wok gently fry the spring onion whites for 2 minutes. Add the belly pork and the mushrooms followed by the stock. Add the sauces and the wine and carefully add the eel. Place the garlic on top and bring to a gentle boil and simmer for 15–20 minutes.

6. Taste and correct the seasoning. Thicken if necessary. Add a dash of white pepper and sesame oil. Spoon out onto a serving dish, sprinkle with some chopped spring onion greens and serve.

Measurements	Ingredients
1 large (approx. 2 lb)	Eel
	Plain flour
2 heads	Whole garlic cloves (peeled)
6 oz	Roast belly pork
	Oil for deep-frying
2 tsp	Potato starch
1 whole	Tangerine peel (soaked in hot water)
6	Spring onions, whites and green separated (chop and reserve for garnish)
4oz 12	Straw mushrooms or Prepared dry Chinese mushrooms
10 fl oz	Chicken stock
1 tbsp	Dark soy sauce
1 tbsp	Light soy sauce
1 tbsp	Oyster sauce
2 tbsp	Shao Xing wine
	Potato starch and water to thicken
	Salt to taste
Dash	Sesame oil
Dash	White pepper

Braised Shoulder of Lamb with Dried Beancurd

Method

1. Bring a wok of water to the boil. Blanch the lamb for 2 minutes, drain. In a hot wok, no oil added, add the lamb and sear until lightly coloured. Place the lamb into a bowl and add the wine, ginger juice, five-spice powder, white pepper and sesame oil. Mix thoroughly and leave for 1–2 hours. This process helps to rid the lamb of some of the rank odour many Chinese find offensive.

2. Heat a wok half full of oil to around 160–170° C. Break the beancurd sticks into thirds if they are too long to fit into the wok. Quickly deep-fry them until they are puffed up, but not brown. Drain and place into a bowl. Cover with boiling water, then cover and leave to soften.

3. In a wok gently fry the chopped clove of garlic in the oil. Add the fermented red beancurd and fry until dry. Add the lamb, water chestnuts, sugar, tangerine peel and the drained beancurd sticks. Add the wine and stir for 30 seconds. Add enough water to cover the ingredients and bring to the boil. Turn down the heat and simmer for 45–60 minutes or until the lamb is tender, adding more water if necessary.

4. Once the lamb is tender, if there is a lot of liquid left, reduce this by half by rapid boiling. Taste and correct the seasoning. Thicken with a little potato starch if required. Add a dash of sesame oil and ground white pepper and place into a serving dish. Garnish with coriander leaves and serve hot.

Measurements	Ingredients
1 lb	Shoulder of lamb, cubed
1 tbsp	Shao Xing wine
2 tsp	Ginger juice
$\frac{1}{4}$ tsp	Five-spice powder
Pinch	Ground white pepper
	Sesame oil
	Oil for deep-frying
4–5 sticks	Dried beancurd
1 clove	Garlic (chopped)
2 tbsp	Oil
$1\frac{1}{2}$ squares	Fermented red beancurd (mashed)
8–10	Water chestnuts (halved)
1 tbsp	Sugar
1 piece	Tangerine peel (soaked and cut into 4 pieces)
2 tbsp	Shao Xing wine
	Salt to taste
	Potato starch and water for thickening
Dash	Sesame oil and ground white pepper
	Fresh coriander leaves for garnish

Ma Po Beancurd

Measurements	Ingredients
2 tbsp	Oil
3 cloves	Garlic (chopped)
4 oz	Marinated pork (chopped)
1 medium	Bamboo shoot (chopped and blanched)
12–15	Water chestnuts (chopped)
2 tbsp	Chilli bean sauce (Toban Jiang)
1 tbsp	Chilli oil
$\frac{1}{2} - \frac{3}{4}$ ladle	Stock
16 oz	Bean curd (pressed then cut into cubes)
	Dark soy sauce
1 tbsp	Oyster sauce
	Salt, sugar and pepper to taste
	Potato starch and water for thickening
Dash	Sesame oil
3	Spring onions (chopped)

Method

1. Heat a wok to a high heat and add the oil. Add the garlic and quickly fry the pork until separated. Add the bamboo shoot, water chestnuts, chilli bean sauce and chilli oil. Stir around thoroughly.

2. Add the stock so that it is level with the top of the meat and add the beancurd. Bring to a fast simmer and stir occasionally to prevent sticking. Be careful not to break the beancurd. Cook for 5 minutes, taste and correct the colour and seasoning. Thicken with potato starch if necessary. Add a dash of sesame oil.

3. Scoop onto a shallow dish and sprinkle with the chopped spring onions.

Lohan Vegetables (1)

Method

1. In a wok, heat the oil. Fry the ginger quickly for 30 seconds and then add the carrot and the bamboo shoot. Stir around for 30 seconds, then add the remaining vegetables.

2. Cook for a minute then add water just level to the ingredients. Add the salt, sugar, dark soy to colour and the vegetarian oyster sauce to taste. Bring to the boil and simmer for 15–20 minutes.

3. Taste and correct the seasoning. Add the glass noodles and cook for 1 more minute. Thicken with potato starch if required. Add a dash of sesame oil and white pepper and serve hot.

Chef's Notes

- You can substitute 1 square fermented red beancurd in place of the dark soy sauce and oyster sauce for a variation.

Measurements	Ingredients
3 tbsp	Oil
1 tbsp	Ginger (chopped)
$\frac{1}{2}$ large	Carrot (peeled and thickly sliced)
$\frac{1}{2}$ tin	Bamboo shoots (thickly sliced and blanched)
6–8	Chinese mushrooms (tinned or reconstituted)
1 oz	Dry lily buds (soaked for 30 minutes)
1 oz	Wood ear (soaked for 1 hour)
$\frac{1}{4}$ tin	Straw mushrooms
10–12	Water chestnuts
2 oz	Fresh or tinned wheat gluten
10–12	Gingko nuts
2 tbsp	Black hair moss (soaked for 30 minutes then blanched)
	Salt
	Sugar
	Dark soy sauce
	Vegetarian oyster (mushroom) sauce
1 bowl	Soaked glass noodles (agar-agar)
	Potato starch and water for thickening
	White pepper and sesame oil

Lohan Vegetables (2)

Method

1. Drain the salt and sour mustard greens from the tin and shred. Squeeze out as much of the brine as possible and then place into a bowl of cold water for 30 minutes to remove the excess brine.

2. Drain off the water and squeeze dry the mustard greens. Place them into the wok and gently heat up, stirring all the time. Bring the wok up to a medium heat and continue to cook the mustard until it looks dry but not burnt. Quickly add half of the oil and sugar and cook until the sugar has melted and coated the mustard. Remove to a plate and cool.

3. Open and drain the liquid from the sweet and sour mustard and set aside. This one needs no additional treatment.

4. In a wok, add the remaining oil then add the ginger and fry for 1 minute before adding the mashed fermented red beancurd. Cook the beancurd until it is dry, then add all the vegetables except the mustards. Cook for about 1 minute before adding the stock or water.

5. Bring to a boil and then simmer for about 15–20 minutes until the vegetables are cooked and soft and have absorbed all the flavours. Taste and correct the seasoning and colour. Add the mustards. Stir around and taste and correct the seasonings again. Thicken slightly, add a dash of sesame oil and white pepper and serve hot.

Measurements	Ingredients
20 oz tin	Salt and sour mustard greens
4 tbsp	Oil
2 tbsp	Sugar
6 oz tin	Sweet and sour mustard greens
2 slices	Ginger
$\frac{1}{2}$ cube	Fermented red beancurd (mashed)
1 oz	Dried wood ear (soaked and trimmed)
$\frac{1}{2}$ tin	Bamboo shoots (thickly sliced and blanched)
12	Gingko nuts
1 oz	Dried lily buds (soaked and trimmed)
10–12 slices	Carrot (thickly sliced and blanched)
16 fl oz	Vegetable stock or water
	Sugar and salt to taste
	Dark soy sauce to colour
	Potato starch and water for thickening
Dash	White pepper and sesame oil

Braised Beancurd Rolls

Method

1. Combine all the filling ingredients in a bowl and mix well. Divide the mixture into 9 portions and use to fill the beancurd skins in the manner of a spring roll. Remember to seal with water/flour paste.

2. Heat a wok half full of oil to 170°–180° C. Quickly deep-fry the rolls in the oil to puff them up and to brown. Drain and set aside.

3. Prepare the braising sauce. Quickly fry the ginger in the oil. Add the stock, oyster sauce, soy sauces, sugar, wine and a pinch of salt. Bring to the boil and add the rolls. Cook, covered, on a low simmer for 10–15 minutes.

4. Remove the lid. If a lot of liquid remains, reduce by fast boiling. Taste and correct the seasoning. Thicken with potato starch if required. Add a dash of sesame oil and white pepper. Serve hot.

Measurements	Ingredients
1½ circles	Beancurd skin (cut into 9 triangles)
	Flour and water paste to seal
	Oil for deep-frying
Filling	Ingredients
8 oz	Chicken (marinated and in strips)
6–8	Chinese mushrooms (shredded)
2 oz	Belly pork (marinated and chopped)
1	Spring onion (chopped)
1 tbsp	Coriander (chopped)
½	Chinese liver sausage (finely diced)
½	Chinese pork sausage (finely diced)
2 slices	Ginger (minced)
Sauce	Ingredients
2 slices	Ginger (shredded)
1 tbsp	Oil
16 fl oz	Stock
2 tbsp	Oyster sauce
1 tsp	Dark soy sauce
2 tsp	Light soy sauce
1½ tsp	Sugar
1 tbsp	Shao Xing wine
	Salt to taste
	Potato starch and water for thickening
Dash	White pepper and sesame oil

Red Braised Ribs

Method

1. Fry the ribs in a wok with the oil until nicely brown. Add the garlic, ginger and chilli, and cook until the garlic and ginger begin to brown.

2. Add the five-spice powder and white pepper and cook until you can smell the five-spice powder. Add the Shao Xing wine, yellow rock sugar and light soy sauce and cook until the alcohol has burned off.

3. Add water to cover and bring to boil, turn down the heat and simmer until the ribs are tender. If there is a lot of liquid remaining, bring to a fast simmer and reduce until just syrupy.

4. Taste, correct seasoning, and if necessary, intensify the colour with some dark soy sauce. Add a dash of white pepper and sesame oil and serve hot.

Measurements	Ingredients
1 lb	Pork ribs
2 tbsp	Oil
2 cloves	Garlic
2 thick slices	Ginger
1	Red chilli, split down the middle, with seeds removed
$\frac{1}{4}$ tsp	Five-spice powder
$\frac{1}{4}$ tsp	Ground white pepper
2 tbsp	Shao Xing wine
2 oz	Yellow rock sugar
2 tbsp	Light soy sauce
	Water
	Dark soy sauce to colour
	Sesame oil
	Ground white pepper

Chinese-style Stewed Brisket of Beef (1)

Measurements	Ingredients
2 lb	Brisket of beef (cubed)
2 tbsp	Oil
2 slices	Ginger (crushed)
2 cloves	Garlic (crushed)
1 tbsp	Sugar
3 tbsp	Braising sauce (see page 60)
	Water
	Potato starch and water for thickening
	Sesame oil
	White pepper

Method

1. Blanch the cubed brisket in boiling water for 2 minutes and drain.

2. Heat the wok, add the oil and fry the ginger and garlic, then add the brisket and cook for a further 2 minutes. Add the sugar and cook until melted, add the braising sauce and cook for a further 2 minutes.

3. Add water to cover the meat and bring to the boil. Turn down the heat and simmer until tender. Taste and correct the seasoning. If necessary, reduce the cooking liquor before correcting the seasoning.

4. Thicken with a touch of potato starch mixed with water if necessary, add a dash of white pepper and sesame oil and serve hot with chilli oil.

Chinese-style Stewed Brisket of Beef (2)

Method

1. Blanch the cubed brisket of beef in boiling water for 2 minutes and drain.

2. Fry the brisket in a little oil with the ginger and garlic. Add the sugar and cook until melted. Add the salt.

3. Add water to cover the meat then add the white pepper, dark soy sauce to colour and the spices in the muslin bag.

4. Bring to the boil and simmer for $1\frac{1}{2}$–2 hours or until tender, skimming constantly. Remove the spices, taste and correct the seasoning and thicken if necessary. Add a dash of sesame oil and serve hot with English mustard or chilli oil.

Measurements	Ingredients
2 lb	Brisket of beef (cubed)
2 tbsp	Oil
2 slices	Ginger (crushed)
2 cloves	Garlic (crushed)
2 oz	Sugar
$\frac{1}{4}$ tsp	Salt
	Water
	White pepper
	Dark soy sauce for colour adjustment
2 tbsp	Spice potting mix tied in muslin bag
	Potato starch and water for thickening
Dash	Sesame oil

Chef's Notes

• Many restaurants include mooli or Chinese radish in this stew. It has quite a sulphurous smell. Add 1 lb peeled and cubed to the above ingredients.

• Spice potting mix is a mixture of star anise, grass fruit, dried liquorice root, dried ginger root, Sichuan peppercorns, cloves and cassia bark. It can be bought in most Chinese supermarkets.

Rice Dishes

15

Rice Congee (Rice Porridge)

Method

1. Wash rice thoroughly and drain.

2. Place rice into a bowl and add the salt and the oil. Mix well. Cover and leave overnight.

3. In a large pan, bring the water to the boil. Add the rice and bring back to a fast boil and turn down the heat so that the water maintains a good motion. The rice should be continuously moving and not settling on the bottom, where it will stick and burn.

4. Boil the rice until the grains fall apart and form rice 'flowers' (around 1½–2 hours). At this stage the congee should be the consistency of soup. If it is too thin, reduce to the correct consistency by fast boiling. If too thick, dilute with boiling water, never cold.

Measurements	Ingredients
6 oz	Rice, preferably Thai fragrant
2 tsp	Salt
3 tbsp	Oil
7 pints	Water

Chef's Notes

• This congee can be eaten plain with fried dough or used as a base for the various different flavoured congees.

Rice Congee Quick Version – 'Rice Sand' Congee

Method

1. In a large pan, bring the water to a fast boil. Using your hands, sprinkle in the ground rice. Allow the water to come back up to the boil before adding an additional handful.

2. Once all the rice has been added, simmer until the rice is cooked and thickened to the consistency of soup.

3. This easy congee can also be used in the various kinds of congee.

Measurements	Ingredients
7 pints	Water
6 oz	Rice, preferably Thai fragrant, ground in a coffee grinder into sand-sized particles, hence the name

Chicken Congee

4 covers

Method

1. Place the chicken into a large bowl and add all the marinade ingredients. Add the oils last of all. Leave to marinate overnight.

2. To prepare the sauce place the ginger into a bowl, heat the oil until smoking and pour over the ginger. Add the remaining ingredients and mix well. Set aside.

Measurements	Ingredients
3½ pints	Congee
1½ lb	Chicken, cut through the bone into bite-sized pieces
Marinade	**Ingredients**
3 heaped tsp	Potato starch
1½ tsp	Salt
1 tsp	Sugar
¼ tsp	White pepper
4 slices	Ginger (shredded)

continued over →

3. In a wok or large pan, heat the congee until boiling. Add the chicken and stir to separate the pieces. Gently bring back to the boil then turn the heat down so that it barely bubbles. Poach the chicken for 10–15 minutes until cooked. Stir occasionally to prevent sticking.

4. If too thick, add some boiling water to thin down. Taste and correct the seasoning. Serve hot in large soup bowls. Serve the dipping sauce in a separate bowl.

...continued

4 cloves	Garlic (peeled and sliced)
2 tbsp	Oil
Dash	Sesame oil
Dipping sauce	Ingredients
4 slices	Ginger (shredded)
4 tbsp	Oil
8	Spring onions (shredded)
1	Red chilli (deseeded and sliced)
Pinch	Ground white pepper
6 tbsp	Light soy sauce
Dash	Sesame oil

Beef Congee

4 covers

Method

1. Place the beef into a bowl and add all the marinade ingredients, the oils last of all. Leave overnight to marinate.

2. Prepare the sauce. Set aside.

3. In a wok or large pan, bring the congee to a boil. Turn down the heat to a gentle simmer and add the beef. Stir with chopsticks to separate. Bring back to a gentle boil, then turn down the heat and poach the beef for 4–5 minutes until cooked.

4. Adjust the consistency if too thick. Taste and correct the seasoning.

5. Serve hot in deep soup bowls with the sauce.

Measurements	Ingredients
$3\frac{1}{2}$ pints	Congee
1 lb	Beef (cut into slices)
Marinade	Ingredients
2 tsp	Potato starch
1 tsp	Salt
1 tsp	Sugar
$\frac{1}{4}$ tsp	White pepper
$\frac{1}{8}$ tsp	Bicarbonate of soda
2 tsp	Soy sauce
1 tsp	Rose liqueur
2 tbsp	Water
2 tbsp	Oil
Dash	Sesame oil
	Dipping sauce for serving (see previous recipe)

Seafood Congee

Method

1. Place the prawns and the scallops into a bowl and add the marinade ingredients, leaving the oils until last. Leave to marinate for 30–60 minutes. The squid does not need to be marinated – the marinade mixture will not stick to the flesh.

2. Prepare the sauce. Set aside.

3. In a large wok or saucepan, bring the congee to a gentle boil. Add the prawns and scallops, stir to separate. Add the squid. Bring back to a boil then remove from the heat. The seafood is now cooked.

4. Serve in deep soup bowls with the sauce.

Measurements	Ingredients
16 (approx. 6 oz)	Prawns (raw, shelled and de-veined)
6	Scallops (each sliced into 4 rounds)
$3\frac{1}{2}$ pints	Congee
1 large	Squid tube scored on the inside, and cut into strips
Marinade	**Ingredients**
1 tsp	Potato starch
1 tsp	Salt
Pinch	Sugar
Pinch	White pepper
2 tbsp	Oil
Dash	Sesame oil
	Dipping sauce for serving (see pages 160–1)

Sea Bass Congee

Method

1. Place the sea bass into a bowl and add the marinade ingredients, the oils last of all. Leave to marinate for 1 hour.

2. Prepare the sauce. Set aside.

3. Portion up the sea bass and place in a layer in four soup bowls. Bring the congee to a fast boil and ladle the boiling congee over the fish slices. Gently push the fish slices with chopsticks to prevent them sticking to the bowls. Cover for 1–2 minutes.

4. Serve immediately with the sauce.

Measurements	Ingredients
$3\frac{1}{2}$ pints	Congee
1 lb	Sea bass fillets (double cut)
$\frac{1}{2}$ tsp	Potato starch
$\frac{1}{2}$ tsp	Salt
Pinch	Sugar
Pinch	White pepper
1 tbsp	Oil
Dash	Sesame oil
	Dipping sauce for serving (see pages 160–1)

Lettuce Congee

4 covers

Measurements	Ingredients
$3\frac{1}{2}$ pints	Congee
1 large	Romaine lettuce (washed and shredded)
4 slices	Ginger (shredded)
4 oz	Preserved Sichuan vegetable (chopped)
	Salt
	Ground white pepper
	Sesame oil

Method

1. In a wok or large pan, bring the congee to a boil. Add the lettuce, preserved vegetable and ginger.

2. Bring back to the boil and simmer for 2–3 minutes until the lettuce is just cooked. Taste and correct the seasoning. Add a dash of sesame oil and serve hot in deep soup bowls.

Congee with Pork and Prawn Balls

Method

1. Place the pork, prawns and Sichuan vegetable into a bowl. Add all the marinade ingredients, except the oils, and mix well. Add the oils and stir the mixture vigorously until it becomes sticky. Gather up the mixture and throw it back into the bowl until it becomes firm. Cover and leave overnight.

Measurements	Ingredients
$3\frac{1}{2}$ pints	Congee
12 oz	Pork meat, finely chopped (meat/fat ratio 80/20)
4 oz	Prawn meat (crushed and finely chopped)
4 tbsp	Preserved Sichuan vegetable (chopped)

continued over →

...continued

2. In a wok or large saucepan, bring the congee to a fast boil. Make balls with the pork and prawn paste and drop into the congee. Turn down the heat and simmer for 5–6 minutes or until the balls are floating. Taste and correct the seasoning. Serve in deep soup bowls with the sauce.

Marinade	Ingredients
2 tsp	Potato starch
1 tsp	Salt
$\frac{1}{2}$ tsp	Sugar
Pinch	Bicarbonate of soda
$\frac{1}{4}$ tsp	White pepper
2 tbsp	Water
2 tsp	Oil
Dash	Sesame oil
	Dipping sauce for serving (see pages 160–1)

Egg Fried Rice (Base Dish)

Measurements	Ingredients
1 small	Egg (beaten with a pinch of salt and pepper)
6–8 oz	Cooked rice per person
	Salt and pepper and soy sauce to taste
Dash	Sesame oil
1 tbsp	Spring onion, chopped (optional)

Method

1. Heat a wok to a medium heat. Add a little oil to coat the wok. Add the egg and scramble quickly. Add the rice and stir-fry until steaming. Taste and correct seasoning. Serve hot with other main dishes.

Variations

- Chicken Fried Rice: Add (per person) 2oz chopped cooked chicken and a handful of defrosted green peas.
- Beef Fried Rice: Add (per person) 2oz chopped cooked Chinese marinated beef, and a handful of defrosted green peas.
- Pork Fried Rice: Add (per person) 2oz chopped barbecue pork and a handful of defrosted green peas.
- Shrimp Fried Rice: Add (per person) 2oz cooked frozen shrimp and a handful of defrosted green peas.
- Prawn Fried Rice: Add (per person) 6–8 prawns (depending on size) (approx. 2oz) and a handful of defrosted green peas.
- Special Fried Rice: Add (per person) 3oz special fried rice mix, which consists of: chopped cooked chicken, cooked shrimps, peas and chopped barbecue pork in equal amounts.

Glutinous Rice 'Chicken'

Method

1. Mix the roughly chopped pork with the marinade. Set aside for 30 minutes.

2. In a hot wok, add the oil and the garlic. Fry until aromatic, then add the marinated pork. Cook until separated and opaque. Add the soaked dried shrimps and cook until fragrant.

3. Add the mushrooms, bamboo shoots and water chestnuts. Cook for 30 seconds. Add the stock and bring to the boil. Add the seasoning ingredients and the shrimp water. Taste and correct the seasoning. Thicken to jam consistency with the water chestnut starch and then add a dash of sesame oil and white pepper. Spread onto a plate to cool quickly.

Measurements	Ingredients
3 oz	Pork (roughly chopped)
1 tbsp	Oil
1 small clove	Garlic (minced)
1 tbsp	Dried shrimps, soaked in hot water. Save water.
3	Chinese mushrooms (soaked and diced)
2 tbsp	Bamboo shoots (chopped and blanched)
4	Water chestnuts (chopped)
$\frac{1}{4}$ pint	Stock
$\frac{1}{2}$ tsp	Dark soy sauce

continued over →

4. Divide the rice into two portions. Blot dry the lotus leaf and lay out on a clean surface. Place one portion of the rice on the lower third of the leaf and mould to form a square about 6 × 6 inches. Spread half the pork mixture onto the rice, leaving an edge of $\frac{1}{2}$ inch, then add the other meats in a thick layer.

5. Spoon the remaining pork mixture over the meats and cover with the remaining half of the rice in a similar sized square. Press lightly at the edges to seal.

6. Roll up the parcel in the lotus leaf as tightly as possible, taking care not to burst it, with the flap on the bottom.

7. Place onto a heatproof rack or plate and steam for 45–60 minutes until piping hot all the way through and the meats are nice and soft.

Chef's Notes

- This is enough for two hungry people, or four as part of dim sum lunch.

...continued

1 tbsp	Oyster sauce
1 tsp	Sugar
	Salt to taste
	Water chestnut starch mixed with water for thickening
Dash	Sesame oil
Dash	White pepper
20 oz	Glutinous rice (cooked)
1 large	Dried lotus leaf (soaked in hot water)
2 thick slices	Char siu
$\frac{1}{2}$	Chinese pork sausage
1 large piece	Roast duck
2 thick slices	Roast belly pork
Marinade	Ingredients
$\frac{1}{2}$ tsp	Potato starch
$\frac{1}{8}$ tsp	Salt
Pinch of each	Sugar, pepper, bicarbonate of soda
1 tbsp	Water
1 tsp	Oil

Glutinous Rice with Preserved Meats

Measurements	Ingredients
10 oz	Glutinous rice
2–3	Braised Chinese mushrooms
$\frac{1}{2}$	Wind-dried Chinese sausage
$\frac{1}{2}$	Wind-dried Chinese liver sausage
2 oz piece	Wind-dried belly pork
	Spring onions (chopped)
	Soy sauce

Method

1. Wash the rice thoroughly and cover with water. Soak for a minimum of 6 hours or overnight. This enables the rice to cook quicker.

2. Drain the rice in a colander or sieve.

3. Place the rice into a suitable ceramic bowl or sand pot, add water or stock so that it is about 5mm above the surface of the rice.

4. Place the mushrooms and the preserved meats on top of the rice and cover loosely with foil.

5. Steam for about 20–25 minutes. Test to see if the rice is cooked by picking out a few grains from the centre and tasting them.

6. To serve, sprinkle over the spring onions and soy sauce. Place the lid on the sand pot and place onto a plate.

Chef's Notes

- Accompaniments should be soy sauce, pickled vegetables.

Noodles

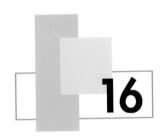

16

Chow Mein: How to Prepare from Dried Noodles

Method

1. Fill the wok to two-thirds full with water. Bring to a fast boil and drop in the noodles, turn off the heat and quickly separate the noodles with a pair of wooden chopsticks. Once they are loose and fully separated, cover and leave for 10 minutes, then pour into a colander and cover with a clean cloth. This is to allow the noodles to steam and finish off the cooking process.

Measurements	Ingredients
½ large (dry weight 3 oz)	Noodle 'cake' per portion/person
2 small (dry weight 3 oz)	Noodle 'cakes' per portion/person

Rice Vermicelli

Method

1. See Chow Mein method.

Measurements	Ingredients
3 oz	Dry noodles per portion

Yi Noodles

Method

1. In a wok or large pan, bring the stock to a boil. If necessary, break the yi noodle round into quarters and place into the stock. Cook until just softened, then remove. Drain and set to one side for later use.

Measurements	Ingredients
1	Yi noodle round per 2 persons
$3\frac{1}{2}$ pints	Light stock, seasoned

2. Skim the oil from the noodles from the top of the stock. This stock can be used later.

Chef's Notes

- Yi noodles are a deep-fried egg noodle. Because of its cooking process, it has large sponge-like pores, which are capable of absorbing a great deal of liquid and, hence, flavours. If the noodles were softened in water and then later reheated in a good superior stock/soup, the water retained by the noodles would then dilute the stock. Thus additional seasoning would be required, which would increase the cooking time of the noodles, which in turn could lead to overcooking.

- These noodles should only be softened in the stock, never boiled, as this would break them up.

Ho Fun with Beef and Peppers in Black Bean Sauce

Measurements	Ingredients
1 lb bag	Fresh ho fun
6 oz	Beef topside (sliced and marinated)
	Oil for blanching beef
2 tbsp	Oil
½ medium	Onion (cut into squares)
1	Green pepper (deseeded and cut into squares)
2 tbsp	Black bean sauce for stir-frying
Little	Stock
Dash	Sesame oil

... a plate.

... run the beef through the oil to partially cook it. Remove and

... the wok and fry the onions and peppers. Add in the ho fun and ... e ho fun to rest on the wok for any length of time as it will stick.

4. Add the beef and the black bean sauce and stir around. Add a little stock if it looks a touch too dry or sticks. Cook for a further 1–2 minutes, add a dash of sesame oil and serve hot.

Crispy Noodles

Method

1. Spread out the noodles onto a plate or tray. Heat a clean wok with the oil until medium hot. Add the noodles carefully in a layer.

2. Gently fry the noodles, turning and moving them to get them crispy and golden on all sides.

Measurements	Ingredients
6 oz	Prepared egg noodles per person
3–4 tbsp	Oil

3. Remove and place onto a tray with lots of kitchen paper to drain. Keep warm in an oven until required.

Crispy Noodles with Mixed Seafood

Measurements	Ingredients
4 stems	Gai lan, washed and each cut into 3–4 pieces
1 small	Squid tube, scored and cut into strips
2 tbsp	Oil
1 tsp	Ginger shreds
1 tsp	Garlic, minced
5	Prawns, shelled, de-veined, butterflied, marinated with a pinch salt, white pepper, 2 pinches potato starch and 1tsp oil
3	Scallops with corals, split if necessary
2	Spring onions (cut into diagonals)
	Salt and pepper to taste
1 tbsp	Shao Xing wine
1 ladle	Stock
1 tbsp	Oyster sauce
	Potato starch for thickening
Dash	Sesame oil and white pepper
6 oz	Crispy noodles

Method

1. Quickly blanch the gai lan in salted water. Then dip the squid into the water so that they just curl up. Remove and drain.

2. Into a hot wok, add the oil and swirl around, add the ginger followed by the garlic. Add the prawns, cook for 30 seconds, add the scallops, cook for 30 seconds, add the spring onions, gai lan and a pinch salt followed by the wine. Cook until it all evaporates.

3. Add the hot stock and cook for 30 seconds. Add the oyster sauce then the squid. Taste and correct the seasoning. Thicken with the potato starch. Turn off the heat, add a dash of white pepper and sesame oil.

4. Place the noodles on a plate, leaving a small dip in the centre. Scoop over the mixed seafood, making sure that the noodles are covered with the sauce. Serve hot.

Crispy Noodles with Shredded Pork and Beansprouts

Method

1. Place pork into a bowl, add the marinade ingredients. Mix well and cover. Place into a fridge for 2–3 hours.

2. In a hot wok with half the oil, cook the shredded pork with the garlic for 1 minute until separate and about half cooked. Remove to one side. Clean the wok if required.

3. In a clean wok, add the remaining oil and heat until very hot. Add the beansprouts with a pinch of sugar and salt. Cook for 30–45 seconds then add the hot stock and wine. Bring to the boil then add the pork and oyster sauce.

4. Cook for 1 minute, taste and correct the seasoning. Thicken with the potato starch, add the onions and turn off the heat. Add a dash of sesame oil and white pepper.

5. Place the noodles onto a plate. Make a small dip in the centre and pour over the pork and beansprouts. Serve hot.

Measurements	Ingredients
6 oz	Pork (thinly shredded)
4 tbsp	Oil
1 clove	Garlic (minced)
6 oz	Beansprouts
	Salt to taste
	Sugar
1 ladle	Hot stock
2 tbsp	Shao Xing wine
2 tbsp	Oyster sauce
	Potato starch for thickening
2	Spring onions (cut into $\frac{3}{4}$ inch batons)
Dash	Sesame oil and white pepper
6 oz	Crispy noodles
Marinade	Ingredients
$\frac{1}{2}$ tsp	Potato starch
$\frac{1}{4}$ tsp	Salt
$\frac{1}{4}$ tsp	Sugar
1 tsp	Wine
$\frac{1}{8}$ tsp	Bicarbonate of soda
Pinch	White pepper
2 tbsp	Water
2 tsp	Oil

Dan Dan Noodles

Measurements	Ingredients
8 oz	Pork (finely minced)
	Water
2 tsp	Salt
2 large or 4 small	Bok choi (washed)
12 oz	Dried noodles
3 tbsp	Oil
3 large cloves	Garlic (finely chopped)
20 fl oz	Stock
Marinade	Ingredients
$\frac{1}{2}$ tsp	Salt
$\frac{1}{2}$ tsp	Potato starch
1 tbsp	Dark soy sauce
1 tbsp	Shao Xing wine
2 tsp	Sesame oil
Sauce	Ingredients
1 tbsp	Sesame paste
1 tbsp	Chilli oil and sediment
1 tbsp	Sesame oil
1 tsp	Sichuan peppercorns (roasted and ground)
2 tsp	Rice vinegar
1 tbsp	Dark soy sauce

Method

1. Place the chopped pork in a bowl and add the marinade ingredients. Mix well and cover. Leave in the fridge for 30 minutes.

2. Mix all the sauce ingredients in a bowl and set aside.

3. Set up two woks, each two-thirds full of water. When they come to the boil, in one wok, add 2 teaspoons salt and the bok choi. Blanch for 2 minutes. Remove and drain on kitchen paper.

4. In the other wok, add the noodles and cook until just done. Drain in a colander, cover and keep hot.

5. Heat a clean wok until smoking, add the oil and garlic, then the pork. Cook for 3 minutes until cooked and separate. Scoop into the sauce and set aside.

6. Place the stock into a wok and bring to a boil. Lightly season. Portion out the noodles into four noodle bowls, chop up the bok choi and divide between the four bowls. Top this with equal amounts of the pork and sauce.

7. Carefully pour a quarter of boiling stock down the side of each of the bowls. Serve immediately.

Shanghai Noodles

Measurements	Ingredients
8 oz	Pork (shredded)
6 tbsp	Oil
4	Spring onions (shredded)
1 tbsp	Shao Xing wine
3 tbsp	Dark soy sauce
1 lb	Bok choi or Chinese leaf (shredded)
	Salt to taste
1 lb	Shanghai noodles
Marinade	Ingredients
$\frac{1}{2}$ tsp	Salt
$\frac{1}{2}$ tsp	Sugar
1 tsp	Light soy sauce
1 tsp	Shao Xing wine
1 tsp	Potato starch
1 tbsp	Water
Pinch	Bicarbonate of soda
2 tsp	Sesame oil

Method

1. Place the pork into a bowl, add the marinade and mix well. Add the sesame oil last. Cover and leave for 30 minutes.

2. Heat 2 tablespoons oil in a wok until smoking, add the pork and stir-fry to separate. Then add the spring onion and cook for 30 seconds, then add the wine. Once the wine is cooked off add 1 tablespoon dark soy sauce, mix well and scoop onto a plate. Clean the wok.

3. Reheat the wok and add 2 tablespoons oil, swirl until smoking. Add the shredded bok choi or Chinese leaf and a pinch or two of salt. Cook until the greens begin to sweat. Cover and turn down the heat. Cook until just tender. Scoop out onto a plate. Clean the wok.

4. Reheat the wok and add the remaining oil. Heat until smoking. Add the noodles and stir-fry until hot. Add the pork and the greens and cook until hot through. Add the remaining dark soy sauce, stir to coat and scoop onto a large plate and serve hot.

Singapore Noodles/Malaysian Chow Mein

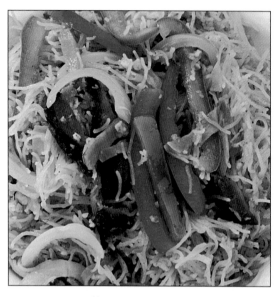

Measurements	Ingredients
3 tbsp	Oil
1	Egg (beaten with seasoning)
4–6 oz	Shredded vegetables and cooked meats, i.e. carrot, peppers, onions, mange tout, beansprouts, ham, roast duck, shrimps, char siu
$\frac{1}{2}$	Red chilli (sliced)
8–10 oz	Prepared noodles (rice vermicelli)
1 tbsp	Cooked curry powder paste
	Sesame oil
	White pepper to finish
	Salt and pepper to taste
	Spring onion (shredded)

Method

1. Add the oil to a hot wok, add the beaten egg and scramble quickly.

2. Add the vegetables and cook for 1 minute until starting to wilt.

3. Add the noodles and meats, maintaining a high heat at all times. Add the curry paste.

4. Toss the noodles constantly to prevent sticking, and cook for around 2–3 minutes until steaming hot.

5. Lower the heat, taste and correct the seasoning. Finish with a dash of sesame oil, white pepper and the shredded spring onion.

Chicken/Beef/Prawn Chow Mein

Method

1. In a hot wok, add the oil, swirl around and add the onions and beansprouts.

2. Cook for 30 seconds, add the noodles and meat/poultry/prawns. Stir around to distribute the meat and vegetables through the noodles.

3. Add half the chow mein sauce and reduce down to nothing. Add half the remaining sauce and reduce to about half.

4. Turn off the heat, taste and correct the seasoning. Add a dash of sesame oil, white pepper and the shredded spring onion. Mix in all the ingredients thoroughly and serve.

Measurements	Ingredients
2 tbsp	Oil
1 oz	Onion (shredded)
1 oz	Beansprouts
8–10 oz	Prepared egg noodles
3 oz	Marinated beef/chicken or
6 (size 26–30)	Marinated prawns, pre-cooked (gone through oil)
4 fl oz	Chow mein sauce (see page 57)
Dash	Sesame oil
	White pepper to finish
1	Spring onion (shredded)

METRIC EQUIVALENTS

Imperial measures are provided throughout this text. Following are the metric equivalents to enable easy conversion.

	Approximate equivalent	Exact equivalent
$\frac{1}{4}$ oz	5 g	7.0 g
$\frac{1}{2}$ oz	10 g	14.1 g
1 oz	25 g	28.3 g
2 oz	50 g	56.6 g
3 oz	75 g	84.9 g
4 oz	100 g	113.2 g
5 oz	125 g	141.5 g
6 oz	150 g	169.8 g
7 oz	175 g	198.1 g
8 oz	200 g	227.0 g
9 oz	225 g	255.3 g
10 oz	250 g	283.0 g
11 oz	275 g	311.3 g
12 oz	300 g	340.0 g
13 oz	325 g	368.3 g
14 oz	350 g	396.6 g
15 oz	375 g	424.0 g
16 oz	400 g	454.0 g
2 lb	1 kg	908.0 g
$\frac{1}{4}$ pt	125 ml	142 ml
$\frac{1}{2}$ pt	250 ml ($\frac{1}{4}$ litre)	284 ml
$\frac{3}{4}$ pt	375 ml	426 ml
1 pt	500 ml ($\frac{1}{2}$ litre)	568 ml
$1\frac{1}{2}$ pt	750 ml ($\frac{3}{4}$ litre)	852 ml
2 pt (1 qt)	1000 ml (1 litre)	1.13 litres
2 qt	2000 ml (2 litres)	2.26 litres
1 gal	$4\frac{1}{2}$ litres	4.54 litres

Index